Different is Not a Disorder

Challenging Childhood Diagnosis:
The Link Between Education and Your Child's Mental Health

Claire T. Russell, MSW, LICSW

Different is Not a Disorder

Different is Not a Disorder

FOR OUR CHILDREN

With gratitude to my colleagues, especially Brianne and Amy; my friends and family who supported me in this endeavor; to Carolyn, my mentor, and to Jarred, without whose technical skills this book would not have been published.

Different is Not a Disorder

CONTENTS

Different is Not a Disorder

PREFACE

I have spent a great deal of time wondering what may have happened to our middle child. I do know that, had I followed the advice of many in the professional community, he would have taken medication; he also may have gone to a school for kids with learning and/or behavioral issues. And what the outcome of all of this would have been, I do not know for certain; I only know what the outcome is of the decisions we did make. Some will read this and say we were just lucky; others may read it and feel inspired to reconsider their approach to their own child's journey. Each parent has to decide what is right for themselves and for their children. On the other hand, I do hope that this book will encourage parents to trust their own instincts and to challenge those whose views do not reconcile with their own experience of their child.

After our youngest entered kindergarten, I made the decision to change careers; prior to having children, I was a public school teacher, but during the time that I had been raising our young family, I developed a desire to help other parents who were struggling with the emotional and practical aftermath of having a child who came into the world with significant challenges. Studies in my Master of Science in Social Work program served to crystallize my focus on children's mental health, and I proceeded to spend twenty-two years practicing in the field, the majority of which were devoted to treating children and families, developing children's programs, and initiating a school-based clinical services model in area public schools.

By the time I became the Director of Children's Services at Community Healthlink in Central Massachusetts, I had developed a deep concern about trends in children's mental health that accounted for the increasing numbers of children with mental health diagnoses, many of whom were also being treated with medication. Fortunately, in our agency, we had a multidisciplinary team approach to assessment and treatment that discouraged this practice, and after years of treating countless children and families, my experience was that very few of the children referred to our clinic legitimately needed the benefit of psychotropic drugs. Instead, many were in circumstances that created the difficulties they were experiencing; in fact, I always felt that it was a tribute to their normalcy that they were responding as they were. My question to those I supervised was, "Why would we expect anything different?"

At the same time, there were children who were in stable home situations who presented their parents or school with the same challenging behaviors, and while these parents may have had more resources or were better equipped to address this challenge, they were not always provided with the options and/or the support they needed to be successful. Although the idea of giving their child medication may not have been the most comfortable solution for them, it could feel like support in a world where they had come to feel powerless as parents and/or had received pressure from their child's school.

As a former teacher in the public schools, I was well aware of the critical role of the child's teacher and his or her learning environment, but it is important to recognize the competing challenges that teachers face in public schools given that standardized measures have increasingly dictated the materials and methods that they are mandated to utilize. This, in turn, demands greater conformity from students in order for these goals to be met; and teachers, who often find themselves on the frontline of children's development along with parents, likely share feelings of frustration that this trend has compromised their ability to adapt to the unique needs of individual students.

In a well-meaning effort to alleviate the concerns of parents and teachers who experience problems with caring for children with challenging behaviors, increasing numbers of children have found their way into the *Diagnostic and Statistical Manual for Mental Disorders*. In some cases, the brains of these children are being studied, and the results are being offered as proof that children who demonstrate certain characteristics have a disorder. The percentage of children taking medication for these diagnosed disorders continues to grow as does the controversy surrounding the validity of the diagnosis itself. For the most part, we have relied on parent and/or teacher reports to make an assessment. And, although an interview of the child, or child and parent together, is usually part of the process, this is an insufficient method for developing an understanding of the child's experience.

Appropriate and required protocols for assessing children and their needs would serve to better identify the underlying causes for children's behaviors. Our current practice demonstrates a lack of understanding about the unique challenges in child assessment as well as the best way to harness and integrate the specific skill sets of each of the professional disciplines involved in children's mental health. While a licensed clinical social worker or a psychologist is not equipped to be managing the medication of a child or adolescent, a psychiatrist or primary care physician may not be in the best position to do a comprehensive assessment of the complex variables inherent in a child's life, not because they don't have the necessary training, but because of the scope of their chosen practice.

What follows is a true story of one child and one family. The variables are many and important. Our second son's constitution and his journey must be appreciated in the context of his parents' constitution and personalities as well as the family constellation in which he found himself. It is a story that is intended to speak to both parents and professionals. For parents, the idea is not that this is what you should do with your child because each child is unique, but by engaging readers with our feelings and reactions as we grappled with the issues that arose throughout our son's life, some parents may experience a sense of kinship and may also find some of the stories amusing as we have all *been there* at one time or another. At the same time, this book will offer an alternative way of thinking about childhood diagnosis and will consider the best way to harness the contributions of scientific research as well as our clinical understanding of psychosocial and temperamentally-based influences.

CHAPTER 1

From the Beginning

There were three in all, two boys and one girl, born within a four-year span. By the time our second son came along (the subject of this book), our eldest was confined to a wheelchair and required visiting nurses and physical therapists. The events that unfolded during those four years resulted in a rollercoaster of emotions: excitement, devastation, hope, disappointment, joy, and denial. We rarely knew what the next day was likely to bring, but we continued to forge ahead to create the family that would be ours.

"This one will be different," were the words spoken by the obstetrician who delivered our second son, knowing full well the history of our first. In the beginning, we delighted in the normal developmental gains of our second child as we had never experienced anything other than one who had multiple physical and mental disabilities. However, our perfect little cherub rather quickly began to exhibit challenging tendencies; long before he had a vocabulary, he was able to communicate an intense dislike of feeling controlled.

"Why does he do that?", my then 35-year old husband would ask. Of course, it seems funny now, watching a 6-foot tall man trying to wrestle what seemed

like an angry rabid bear cub into a car seat and fasten the safety belt. However, the truth is that the anguish and cries that came from this child were actually heart-wrenching to witness, and the frequency and intensity with which our son continued to wage this war was remarkable.

Over time, this became a seemingly intractable pattern that was not limited to our son's relationship with us. That said, at the same time, he was also an active, by all accounts, seemingly happy toddler. He did not have difficulties with sleeping, eating, or playing. He loved to push his little sister, only seventeen months younger, throughout the house in her rolling seat. He was curious and busy, highly energetic, and adorable. We found that letting him run free at the local park was helpful in managing his boundless energy, and despite the fact that it was an intensely busy and hectic household with three children under the age of five, we remember lots of smiles and laughter. We were both exhausted most of the time, but we felt that we were living in a generally happy household, and we enjoyed watching our young children grow and develop, noticing how different they were from each other.

The unique journey of our oldest son would stand in stark contrast to the normal developmental gains of his brother and sister. In those first few years, the seriousness of his limitations would become clear, and although he was unable to walk, talk, or exhibit most purposeful movement, his brother and sister developed a strong bond with him that would last throughout his lifetime. As parents, the juxtaposition of two active, curious, and spirited children with a child who required visiting nurses, physical therapy, and adaptive equipment was a powerful and sad reality; and yet, I have often wondered about how that reality allowed us to take many of our second son's antics in stride.

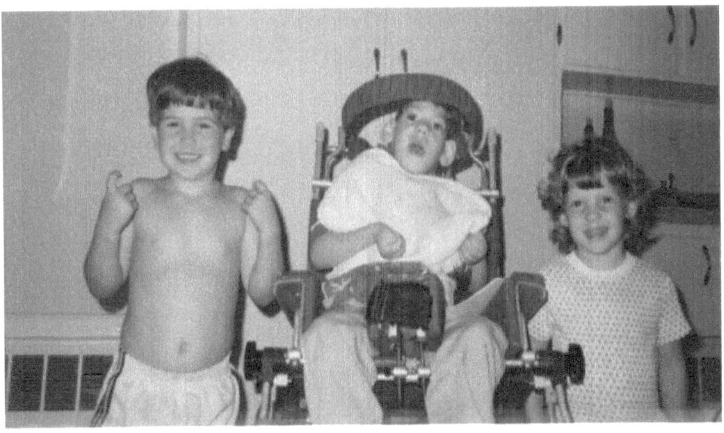

For the most part, I thoroughly enjoyed my temporary role as a stay-at-home mom. I was able to witness and recount many of the funny things they did in their interactions with each other and with me. I was also privy to all of those developmental firsts that might otherwise have been missed. Although admittedly challenging at times, it often felt as though I was provided with a personal source of daily entertainment; in fact, sometimes it seemed a bit like a zoo. It was not unusual to see our youngest swinging from the doorway in her Jolly Jumper, using her feet to push herself as high as she could and, at the same time, our middle child roaming from one toy to another, occasionally batting a Happy Apple around on the tray of his older brother's wheelchair.

Although it may be a wise decision to be a little older when you have children, as many new parents are today, no one can really prepare you for how much your life will change and all of the different ways you may find yourselves being tested. You can't necessarily make predictions because you may not have anything to base them on, particularly with first children or if you have children in rapid succession. And although the vast majority of people become parents at one time or another, there seems to be an assumption that they will somehow know what to do when their children arrive; the truth is that you get far more training in learning how to operate a cash register.

By the time we realized we needed help, we were too exhausted to figure out how to make it happen. Fortunately for us, the solution fell into our laps; as I was juggling a wailing, months-old daughter in my arms (I had walked outside to keep her from waking up my napping whirling dervish), my neighbor offered up her high-school daughter to help out in the afternoons. Of course, since she was the mother of five, several of whom were adolescents, I was suspicious that perhaps she was just trying to thin out the teenage population in her own house, but I was willing to try anything.

Her daughter was amazing: soft-spoken, polite, smart, and admiring of our children. She clearly enjoyed our entourage, and her daily afternoon appearance provided a welcome respite from the day to day demands of our busy household. Her designated role was intended to be a wise playmate rather than a disciplinarian, and despite the customary challenges to authority posed by our second son, she seemed to exact joy and humor from our children's antics. To this point, one of my favorite memories of her is memorialized in a picture I took after returning home from a quick errand having found her sitting on the floor between my two youngest with her hands taped together and a scarf tied around her mouth.

Nursery school was merely the beginning of what would be a long litany of encounters with many of our second son's teachers. The earliest reports reflected exactly what we experienced at home: "He is bright, energetic and happy; he loves to play, especially physically; he is creative; he likes to present at show and tell, and lead the group in song." But there was also this. "He doesn't want help; he tries everything himself; he is at times uncooperative when his will is strong; he says 'no way' a lot, both in fun and in seriousness."

Much of what I reflect on now is the issue of balance as it relates to one's experience in life. Fortunately, our son's positive qualities counterbalanced any challenges he presented, either at home or at school, during those very early years. It was clear that his teachers enjoyed this spirited and determined little boy, and the environment of nursery school provided enough flexibility that, by its very nature, did not present the opportunities for conflict that would increase in the years to come.

Most parents wonder how their children will fare on the school bus, particularly the ones with precocious personalities. The things that our son may have been cute enough to get away with in nursery school did not always work as well on the school bus or in the kindergarten and primary grades. We got our first inkling about this very early on; one day, after disembarking from the bus, the first words out of his mouth were, "Mom, does the bus driver know my phone number?" I thought it was an odd question; somehow, I also knew it was not a good sign. I waited for the call, which, fortunately, never came.

With the benefit of time, I developed a great appreciation for the prophetic nature of kindergarten report cards; there are often endearing categories such as *I can pay attention to stories* and *I can express ideas.* Our son was a standout in *Is active and energetic* but much less so in *Listens and follows directions.* The word behavior had now crept into the parent/teacher conversation, and it came to mean the ability to comply and to do the thing that was required in the moment. The teacher noted that this was an intelligent and curious child who was interested in many things, and that he was eager and enthusiastic as long as he was engaged in something of interest. However, he was resistant to adapting to schedules that required him to engage with a variety of other activities.

Now, the question about why one child would resist this request to conform so intensely, and most do not, is important. What interpretations can one make? If you're the teacher, one strategy that is typically used is to teach the errant kindergartner to conform by punishing the bad behavior and rewarding the good behavior. In my son's case, this meant *Smiley Face* notes or *Frown* notes going home with him every day, but do the smiley faces and the frowns work? Perhaps so, at least in kindergarten and for that day, but what is really being accomplished? Does the non-conforming kindergartner develop new lifelong skills to sit still and be quiet when required or to sing when the other students are singing?

Traditional teaching and learning require that students, even very young students, cover an array of curriculum components regardless of their interest, and much of what is presented must be experienced by all of the students at the same time. Bad behavior, then, becomes defined as anything that is different from what most of the students can more easily do, and good behavior becomes defined as doing just what all of the other students are doing. Kids who exhibit bad behavior get labeled pretty quickly, and they are probably aware that they are going home with *faces* while most of the other children are not.

Besides the potential pitfalls of how the growing child internalizes this process, it doesn't really address the question of why the child is not conforming in the first place. The answer to that question is far more important and too often overlooked. There was a part of me that hated the faces, whether or not they were smiley or they were a frown, because my sense was that a tiny slice of my son, a comparatively much less important slice, had been carved out from him to be molded and modified; I was more concerned about how the rest of him would find optimal expression in an environment where I feared he would increasingly be viewed as a negative influence.

Meanwhile, his little sister was busy developing a strategy for dealing with her strong-willed brother. Who said a toddler couldn't strategize? At first, I did not realize that our daughter had figured out how to *set him up* by doing things that she knew would elicit an inappropriate reaction from him, and he rarely disappointed. The sequence became predictable; it began with her screams, followed by accusations of something he had done that she knew would likely result in his punishment. I had witnessed firsthand many of the encounters between these two children in which my daughter would attempt to explain her position to her brother who, in turn, became increasingly agitated that he simply couldn't make her understand his belief that he was right. He would then *get in her face*, as the expression goes, and although he wouldn't resort to being physical, his body language was definitely intimidating. So, in my mind, of *course,* it was his fault and of *course,* my daughter was the innocent victim, even though I did not always see firsthand what had actually transpired.

Once I had a more realistic grasp on what was happening, I sought to interrupt the pattern without having to monitor, referee, or adjudicate every disagreement. The book, *Siblings Without Rivalry* (Faber & Mazlish,2012), offers clever strategies which outline specific and reasoned steps parents can take to help children learn how to settle their own disputes. It was actually great fun standing outside of the room, listening to their attempts at compromise; like a trainer for prizefighters, I would go in when it seemed that things were beginning to deteriorate and root them on.

Although it definitely improved things between them at that time, the basic themes of control and adaptation to control would continue to be a major variable in their relationship for many years.

Any struggles that we had with our middle son, however, were tempered by the many stories we remember about him in those early years that still make us laugh. Full of life, precocious, and outrageous were just some of the adjectives many used to describe his antics. As an example, when he decided on one particular afternoon that he didn't like the son of a friend of mine who had come for a visit, he simply whipped out what he must have considered to be his most potent weapon and urinated on him! Of course, I offered to launder the child's clothes, but, not surprisingly, mom felt inclined to make a hasty exit and never visited our house again. Likewise, I was equally mortified when I received a telephone call from the school to report that he and a friend (a male, thankfully) were found under a classroom table comparing private parts; it was difficult to know how to respond. One of the skills that many parents find they must develop at one point or another during the course of raising children is how to be humbled gracefully, and fortunately, or perhaps unfortunately for us, we got broken in very early.

By now, a picture had emerged of a very strong-willed child who was bright and precocious, and despite some of his outward behaviors, he was also sweet, sensitive, and affectionate. The reports from school, as well as what we were noticing at home, suggested that he was struggling, but it was not clear how or why. Teachers continued to resort to *faces* and notes going home each day to chronicle his progress or lack thereof. Meanwhile, we were trying the usual things parents try such as time-outs, and occasionally even downright bribes, but he had developed a prolific vocabulary and tried to make what he considered to be reasoned arguments with us about almost anything. It didn't matter how large or small the issue was, it seemed to take on the same critical importance to him. Winning the argument was paramount, and what had now become a somewhat disrespectful pitch caused us to wonder what we may be doing wrong.

A concurrent and sad development related to our oldest son's placement in a pediatric nursing facility; his increasing medical needs resulted in the need for full-time nursing care. It was a devastating development, ameliorated only by our knowledge that he would be well cared for. We arranged for help so that he could be home on weekends and holidays, and despite the fact that he no longer lived at home during the week, he remained an integral part of our family.

We wondered how well each of our younger children were dealing with this emotionally, and whether this development might explain some of our second son's behavior, which had begun to look and feel a bit more like anger. We anticipated that we would need to better understand the source of his disconcerting interactions with us in order to be able to advocate for him in what we feared would become an increasingly contentious environment.

CHAPTER 2

A Strategy That Worked

"What is right is not always popular; what is popular is not always right." - Albert Einstein

By the time our son entered elementary school, here is what we knew for certain. The generally accepted strategies for dealing with oppositional behavior did not work: for him, time out was an opportunity to escape from unjust confinement; redirecting only worked if it was something he wanted to do in the first place, and withholding privileges did not deter him from future attempts to assert his will in the least. We had tried being firm, consistent, and united in our approach, but it seemed that no matter what we tried, it did not change either the course, or the outcome, of the standoff once it began.

For years, professionals who specialize in the field of children's mental health have weighed in on parenting issues specifically as they relate to strong-willed children. One of the widely read child psychologists in the seventies, Dr. James Dobson, author of *The Strong-Willed Child* (2004), proposed that strong-willed children disobeyed their parents specifically to test them, and that the parent(s) needed to level their authority on the child. According to Dr. Dobson, leveling their authority could include physical punishment, such as the use of spankings or a switch. His recommended approach is rooted in the notion that "children are naturally inclined toward rebellion, selfishness, dishonesty, aggression, exploitation, and greed" (p. 46).

Whether you do or don't believe that children are behaving badly just to test you, this is a dangerous theory. Where does the physical punishment stop in the event that the spanking or the switch doesn't work? Well, it turns out that Dr. Dobson has the answer to this too, on page 3, where he tells the story of his twelve-pound dachshund, Siggie (named after Sigmund Freud). He describes the dog as being a 'confirmed revolutionary' and then proceeds to recount the story of Siggie's refusal to go into his bed which was a permanent enclosure in the family room.

> I turned and went to my closet and got a small belt to help me 'reason' with 'ol Sig'...When I returned, I held up the belt and again told the angry dog to get into his bed. He stood his ground so I gave him a firm swat across the rear end, and he tried to bite the belt. I popped him again and he tried to bite me. What developed next is impossible to describe. That tiny dog and I had the most vicious fight ever staged between man and beast. I fought him up one wall and down the other, with both of us scratching and clawing and growling ...Inch by inch I moved him toward the family room and his bed ... I eventually got him into his bed, but only because I outweighed him two hundred to twelve!

In the end, Dr. Dobson proudly proclaimed victory. Upon reading this troubling account, I must confess that I found myself rooting for the dog, and I also wondered how this would have ended had Dr. Dobson's adversary been a 180-pound teenager as opposed to a 12-pound domestic animal. Dr. Dobson proposes that once you gain control of a dog or a child by such a strategy, they will no longer challenge your authority. However, even if one agrees that this can be described as a victory, what is the cost of using such measures?

Unlike a dog, a child's understanding of or reaction to any perceived authority, which is attempted to be leveled in such a cruel manner, will be influenced by the development of his or her reasoning skills as well as the need to feel safety in primary relationships and in the larger community. Furthermore, this primitive approach, which is borne out of fear rather than respect, is likely to engender either an aggressive response from the youngster or a protective distancing in which the parents' attempts to maintain control essentially forsake any meaningful influence.

When our son was just seven years old, we consulted with a child psychologist because we did not believe that any child would go to such lengths to test their parents, and because we wanted a better answer as to the underlying explanation for his behavior. Could it just be inherited personality traits or could there be some unconscious anger about his brother's condition? The psychologist's assessment, which was based on one meeting with us as well as several individual meetings with our son, was that his behavior did not appear to be related to anger regarding his brother. Rather, he observed that our son possessed very strong personality traits, and that he could, and would attempt to defend his opinions relentlessly.

He suggested that we read about and consider the recommended strategies of another well-read child psychologist at the time, Dr. Ross Greene, the founder of a non-profit organization, "Lives in the Balance" and author of *The Explosive Child* (2010). Dr. Greene's research offers an entirely different formulation about strong-willed children, attributing their oppositional behavior to challenges in the areas of cognitive flexibility and frustration tolerance. His theory is based on studies of the brain as well as his clinical work with hundreds of children who responded unfavorably to the interventions that typically work for most parents.

In this model, it is suggested that parenting strategies focus on: reducing the frequency of conflict by limiting discipline to issues relating to safety; adopting a collaborative, problem-solving approach to deal with disagreements that may provide a learning opportunity for the child, and identifying and relinquishing those struggles that are not worthy of a major confrontation. No cattle prods; what a relief!

Ross Greene's "3 Basket" model, which attempts to effectively limit the number of arguments with a child like ours on any given day, turned out to be invaluable. We were advised to include only those behaviors that related to safety (our son's or someone else's) in Basket A. Basket B was to include behaviors that were not worthy of resulting in a full-blown meltdown, but that would provide us with an opportunity to teach or model skills in communication, negotiation, and compromise. Basket C was to include everything else; this basket was intended to be very full with behaviors that, in the grand scheme of things, were deemed not to be that important.

One of the most helpful aspects of this approach is that it shifts the issue away from child blaming or parent blaming and, instead, focuses on the realistic constitutional characteristics of the child that contribute to the struggle. This strategy felt comfortable for me for two reasons: first, it was consistent with my intuition about what was driving my son's behavior, and secondly, I felt that re-establishing a more harmonious atmosphere at home would contribute positively to our relationship with our son and to family life in general.

Furthermore, it was painful to watch how overwhelming it was for my son when a struggle would ensue; the escalating conflict seemed to create an intellectual paralysis that rendered him unable to respond to reason. It was clear to me that this was not some intentional ploy to see what he could get away with, and it was frustrating that the things parents usually do with children in these situations did not work for our son.

It felt risky to be adopting a position that defied conventional wisdom. We had found comfort in using techniques that were consistent with generally accepted norms, and by allowing our child more autonomy than is typical, we knew that we would feel responsible if our approach proved unsuccessful. However, we discovered that there were advantages both for him and for us by relinquishing authority on many of the issues that we otherwise would have addressed.

For example, when he decided to go to the bus stop in cold weather without a jacket, we didn't argue with him. Instead, we adopted the position that if he went outside without a jacket and felt cold while waiting for the bus, he would wear a jacket the next time; it wasn't an argument we needed to have. I can understand that many parents would be less than enamored with this approach, but it worked well for us, and I was unapologetic in deflecting the predictable criticism from those parents for whom the notion of not being in control was intolerable. The number of daily arguments decreased significantly. As well, when our son realized that a decision was his to make, the energy he typically expended in trying to promote his position could become refocused on considering the advantages or disadvantages of one potential choice over another; and now, our limited and unequivocal demands were met with far less resistance.

Our son's determination to make his own decisions was a central theme in his life exacerbated by a general personal attitude that he was always right, and that he could do anything he set his mind to. The combination was potent, and it was made even more so by his high level of sensitivity. One of the many telephone calls we received from the school in those early years came from his second-grade teacher. Learning to write in script was one of the things they had been working on that particular day, and it had become apparent over time that handwriting was not his greatest strength. Although the teacher had merely approached his desk and attempted to correct the grasp of his pencil, he burst into tears. Nothing frustrated our son more than not being able to do something he tried to do, and he was relentless in his efforts if it was something he was motivated to accomplish.

We learned that it was never helpful to point out to him what he couldn't do or needed to do better; such an approach actually had a negative impact because he truly believed that if he wanted to do it, he could, and coming up short was simply not imaginable for him. Some people would refer to this in very simple terms: he's just a child and not understanding. Others would describe it as obstinance or a refusal to acquiesce and accept help. For us, although it was difficult to witness the angst that this quality caused our son, we suspected that this characteristic mostly reflected a strong constitutional trait that could translate into an advantage for him in his adult life.

By the time he entered the third grade, our highly active child was still highly active; his dislike of being controlled had not waned. At the same time, however, there was an increasing need for him to sit still, to quietly pay attention, and to conform to classroom procedures. Words such as disruptive, inattentive, and oppositional were creeping into the conversation, and it seemed as though our son was anxiously aware that he and his teacher were not *simpatico*.

I still remember the telephone call; the guidance counselor wanted to meet with us during our son's parent/teacher conference. I was ready, or at least I thought I was. It should not be surprising that this is a common time that children, particularly boys, find themselves being diagnosed with ADHD and prescribed a trial of medication. By this time, the child has become too old for such techniques as *smiley faces* and *frowns*, and there is an increased need for students to be able to adjust to whatever the teacher needs them to do in the moment. Students have less opportunity for spontaneity, being active, or just generally doing things that are different from what all of the other students are doing. As well, standardized measures of achievement have created pressure upon teachers to ensure that their students meet designated goals. These developments increase the likelihood that children who need flexibility because of learning profile, personality style, or developmental readiness will be viewed negatively.

Much of the justification for the increasing practice of diagnosing and medicating children is rooted in the notion that the child cannot concentrate or pay attention, but I knew that this was not the case for our son. I believed that his lack of willingness to attend to the things the teacher presented likely had more to do with his extremely strong will to concentrate and pay attention only to those things that he found interesting and/or wanted to be doing. At home, we found it nearly impossible to shift his attention away from something in which he was truly engaged.

Not surprisingly, the parent teacher conference became tense. I suggested that using a more flexible approach with our son may alleviate the friction that had developed in the parent/teacher relationship and result in his increased cooperation; however, my suggestion was met with resistance. Predictably, a recommendation was made for an evaluation of attention deficit hyperactivity disorder, and, as parents, we felt pressured to acquiesce. We also wondered whether our reluctance was interpreted as denial or over-protectiveness.

The teacher's unwillingness to consider the potential advantages of a more flexible strategy, similar to the one we had adopted at home. did not bode well for his remaining months in her class. Fortunately, we lived in a school system that solicited input from parents regarding classroom assignments for their children. Therefore, we refocused our energy on advocating for our son's placement in the classroom that we felt may best meet his needs in his fourth-grade year. We also respectfully declined the suggestion to have him evaluated for ADHD.

The irony of all of this was that no one was harder on my son than he was. He imposed high standards on himself which he was driven to meet; and because he felt he could do anything he desired to do with enough effort, he tended to rely solely on himself for his success. As well, it didn't matter who you were or how credentialed you were; if my son thought he knew something, and was convinced that he was right, he could not seem to hear or believe evidence to the contrary.

He was an early tennis player, one of the many sports that he engaged in, and it turned out that his tennis teacher had actually qualified at Wimbledon years earlier; yet, our son found it difficult to take pointers or corrections, even from him! As a memoir of his unwillingness to accept direction, as well as his frustration at losing a game, we still have as evidence the distorted racket that he reported as having *fallen* during one of his group lessons when, in reality, he had slammed it against the floor or net support. Failing at something only generated anger and increased determination in our son; it did not make him think that someone else knew better than he did or that he could be successful with their help.

For many, the idea of flexibility and freedom in schools tends to conjure up notions of underachieving or unruly students who don't know how to set or pursue goals for themselves. Based on this theory, children need to be instructed in the conventional sense and held accountable by quizzing or testing them on the material that they have been presented. However, I believe that this is an erroneous assumption as far as many children are concerned, and particularly as it related to our son.

Fortunately, his fourth-grade teacher presented a very different, more flexible approach to teaching and learning which included a math component that was based entirely on baseball statistics, an area of knowledge familiar to most ten-year old boys. And rather than disparage our son's apparent need for control in making his own decisions, he forged a respectful relationship that allowed him to foster our son's cooperation and willingness to conform when it became necessary.

The basic themes of self-determination and control remained; however, he now had a sensitive and nurturing teacher who did not personalize his behavior. Our son's basic make-up had not changed; what *did* change was his environment. He still had an extremely strong will; he continued to be relentlessly hard on himself and to find it stressful when he didn't do things correctly the first time. His reactions tended to surprise everyone, including us.

We continued to watch with amazement, and sometimes sympathy, but the balance in his life, and ours, had been restored simply by a change in his environment. Now, the lens through which our son was being viewed, as well as the language that was used to describe him, had shifted. He completed elementary school (fifth grade) with high marks, positive reports, and renewed self-esteem; gone were the concerns that had been raised only

two years earlier.

By this time, our household had grown to include a dog and three cats which may not seem very significant, but the reality is that the level of mayhem it created, particularly on weekends when our oldest son was home, actually served to diffuse the inherent tension in the relationship between our middle and youngest children.

Even though overt conflict between them had become much less frequent, the dynamic was familiar.

Our daughter's analytical and verbal skills had increased, and our son was less inclined to be as reactive as he had been in earlier years, but their natural tendencies in dealing with most things in life remained on opposite ends of the spectrum. In fact, our daughter's experience in elementary school actually served to highlight the degree of our son's willfulness. They were both outstanding students, played sports, and had friends, but while our son was busy reshaping tennis rackets, our daughter seemed totally unfazed when she ran the wrong way on the soccer field during a game. It's not that she didn't care about winning or that she wasn't motivated to be a high achiever; she simply did not react with such intensity when unexpected or disappointing things happened. Her tendency was to accept, and to maneuver within, the realities she encountered in life.

Since those early years, I have wondered whether I could have accepted the recommendation of the psychologist we consulted had he proposed that my son receive a trial of medication. The opinion I had already formed was based not only on my observations of my child, but my strong intuition about what was driving his behavior. Issues of temperament and personality can cloud the assessment of a child who demonstrates symptoms of inattention or hyperactivity. This can result in an intense effort to compel the child to conform by inaccurately diagnosing them which, in turn, may lead to inappropriate treatment recommendations. Peter Gray (2013) is a research psychologist, specializing in education, who sums up this dynamic succinctly in his book, *Free to Learn*. "Instead of adjusting to the diversity of personalities, schools try to mold personalities to fit the school, often with drugs. The most obvious current example of this concerns the high rate of diagnosis of ADHD" (p. 81).

In addition to the issue of a child being misdiagnosed or treatment indications unwarranted, there are other concerns for the well-being of any child when they are in an environment where their personal attributes are being maligned. In our son's case, because of his indomitable spirit, his tendency was to fight back and to defend his position. But what happens to the scores of other children who may internalize this lack of understanding from the teacher differently? Do they feel *less than* the other students in the room? Do they withdraw, become depressed, anxious, or develop feelings of incompetence? Do they begin to see themselves in the same way that the teacher sees them?

There is no question that a child's developing sense of self-esteem has much to do with how the adults in their lives view them as well as the feedback they receive from those adults. The ability for them to draw upon their positive attributes is dependent upon a healthy sense of self-esteem, individuality, and motivation for self-determination. Parents know when their children are happy and feel secure. There was a noticeable difference between our son's demeanor during his third-grade year, when the teacher focused primarily on his unwillingness to conform, and his fourth-grade year, when the focus shifted to harnessing our son's strengths to promote personal growth and cooperation.

All too often, ADHD has become a fallback position for those who are trying to understand and deal with challenging behaviors in children, but there are alternative theories to consider regarding the inherent tension between typical characteristics of many third-grade boys and the traditional school classroom. To establish credibility for *any* viewpoint that one may have concerning the debate, it is important to examine all sides of the issue, including recent and relevant studies. By considering the contributions of science, as well as the knowledge base that exists regarding psychosocial contributors, temperament, and child assessment practices, we are in the best position to find common ground on what has become a highly controversial subject.

CHAPTER 3

ADD

<u>A</u>ttention <u>D</u>ifferentiated <u>D</u>evelopment

"The art of medicine consists in amusing the patient
while nature cures the disease." – Voltaire

The controversy surrounding attention deficit hyperactivity disorder and other childhood diagnoses on the disruptive behavior disorder spectrum, such as oppositional defiant disorder and conduct disorder, has become increasingly adversarial. Even for those who are believers, it must be somewhat disconcerting to think that 11-14% of our school-aged children have attention deficit hyperactivity disorder (Centers for Disease Control and Prevention 2017), and it must be equally disconcerting for parents who have struggled, and ultimately decided in favor of medication management, to then have that decision be suspect or discredited.

The qualifying identifiers of attention deficit hyperactivity disorder, outlined in the *Diagnostic and Statistical Manual of Mental Disorders*, which are present in most children at some time and to some degree only serve to polarize the argument for or against. For purposes of this conversation, I am providing the diagnostic criteria here:

ADHD (attention deficit hyperactivity disorder)

Inattentive Type - the child needs to meet six of the following, and they must have been present for at least 6 months:
- Often fails to give close attention to details/makes careless mistakes; trouble holding attention on tasks
- Not listening when spoken to
- Not following through, (getting distracted, sidetracked)
- Trouble organizing tasks/activities
- Avoiding tasks that require mental effort
- Loses things
- Easily distracted
- Forgetful

Hyperactive-impulsive type – the child needs to meet six of the following, and they also must have been present for at least six months:
- Fidgets with or taps hands or feet, or squirms in seat
- Leaves seat without permission
- Runs about or climbs in inappropriate situations
- Unable to take part in leisure activities quietly
- Is often "on the go"
- Talks excessively
- Blurts out answers before question is finished
- Trouble waiting turn

- Interrupts others.

Combined type – the child must have six items from each category present for at least six months.

In addition, the following qualifiers must be met:
- Several inattentive or hyperactive-impulsive symptoms were present before age 12 years.
- Several symptoms are present in two or more setting, such as at home and in school.
- There must be clear evidence that the symptoms interfere with, or reduce the quality of the child's functioning.

I think most of us would agree that all children at one time or another exhibit some of the symptoms of ADHD; therefore, the determining factors in making a diagnosis may come down to the frequency and/or the level of intensity of the behaviors, as well as the level of tolerance one adult may have over another for differences among children. In fact, it may be reasonable to assume that those adults who have more tolerance for normal variation in behaviors among children will find themselves among the non-believers and skeptics.

Some non-believers and skeptics cite variability among children in terms of their energy level and individual need(s) for exercise as evidence of a child's normalcy; to further support such a position, common sense parallels may be invoked. One such example might be that if we accept the idea that a poodle needs more daily exercise than a golden retriever, we should be able to accept the notion that one child may need more exercise than another. Other non-believers, especially those who practice in the field of children's mental health, may also offer evidence of their suspicions by legitimately noting that ADHD is represented more frequently within certain demographics. CDC statistics, which were cited earlier in this chapter, offer several examples: it is diagnosed more than twice as often in boys than in girls; children who are on Medicaid are twice as likely to have the diagnosis, and children in foster care are three times as likely to be diagnosed.

By contrast, those who are proponents of the validity of the ADHD diagnosis point to the results that are obtained when a child is placed on medication. Parents and teachers often notice a reduction in symptoms, and some even say that the symptoms disappear altogether. This certainly can help to alleviate a strained relationship between a parent and a child, or a teacher and a child; at the same time, it may also help a child to have more satisfactory social relationships with peers. Additionally, some believers will cite the growing body of knowledge in neuroscience that exists to explain the relationship between the brain and human behavior. Recent studies suggest that it is the difference in structure or volume within certain areas of a child's brain that is the cause of the child's symptoms.

A comprehensive study of this kind was conducted by a group of scientists from more than nine countries and involved a large sample of both diagnosed children and adults, a total of 3,242 people. The researchers represented investigators from centers throughout the world, including the Netherlands, Australia, United States, Spain, Norway, Demark, Germany, Ireland, and England.

The ENIGMA (Enhancing NeuroImaging Genetics through Meta-Analysis) Collaborative found subcortical volume differences in certain areas of the brain, including the prefrontal lobe, which is believed to be associated with symptoms of attention deficit hyperactivity disorder (Jenco, 2017). The differences between the brains of individuals with ADHD and those without were described as very small, in the range of a few percent. Additionally, these differences in brain structure in the children who were studied were not commensurately represented in the adults in the sample which led this research group to determine that attention deficit hyperactivity disorder is most aptly described as a delay in brain maturation.

The effective result of the myriad of disparate viewpoints regarding the validity and origin of the ADHD diagnosis has been to create a climate of confusion for parents and professionals who are attempting to address presenting challenges with a uniform and accepted standard of care. Therefore, rather than assuming a position for or against, taking steps that can ensure the integrity of an accurate diagnosis should serve to lessen the frequently intractable positions on either side of the argument. Developing a clear understanding of what is driving the child's behavior allows an evaluator to develop a formulation that suggests an appropriate treatment goal, and the child's voice is a critical element in this process.

In order to give voice to very young children, trained therapists use symbolic and creative forms of play to elicit the child's experience of his or her environment. With a reluctant or guarded adolescent or latency-aged child, the therapist may also utilize collaborative board games for the purpose of developing a mutually respectful, non-authoritarian based relationship. These methods, unlike the traditional clinical interview, provide an opportunity for the youngster to share their thoughts and feelings in a non-threatening environment and through developmentally appropriate methods. Unfortunately, this critical step is often overlooked in the current assessment process.

This need to hear directly from the child should not feel threatening to the adults in his or her life; the goal of the therapist is not to collect evidence of a suspected deficiency or transgression on the part of a parent or a teacher. When a child demonstrates behaviors that become concerning to adults, it can be a signal that they are struggling with something in their environment that they have been unable to share.

The unique aspect of child assessment relies on the knowledge and skill of the therapist to discover the underlying cause of the child's presenting behavior, and while there are many disciplines that provide counseling and therapy, the critical question for parents and teachers should be whether the provider has such training; do they concentrate their practice on children and adolescents? Children who are struggling with an emotional reaction to an environmental stressor, and who meet the criteria for ADHD, deserve to have an intervention that is targeted to the cause of the stressor in the child's life. The alternative poses an important ethical argument about children's rights given their age and inability to impact the decisions that are made.

Marilyn Wedge is a child and family therapist who, in her book, *Suffer the Children* (2011), details the case of a young child whose symptoms in school were discovered to be related to the child's concerns about her mother's unhappiness with her job. In this case, the mother had been openly complaining about her feelings of unhappiness and frustration so that, by the time the child left for school, he had become preoccupied with anxious thoughts about her welfare. Children who feel preoccupied and anxious are at high risk for meeting criteria for attention deficit hyperactivity disorder given that anxiety and preoccupation can easily become misinterpreted for hyperactivity and inattention. In this case, an intervention targeted at helping the mother to understand the effect that this was having on her child ultimately resolved the child's symptoms.

In the extreme, there are countless children who, sadly, are being abused and traumatized by the situations in which they live. Diagnosing and medicating them may be tantamount to blaming the victim, especially given that there already exists within the current diagnostic and statistical manual diagnoses for children other than ADHD, such as those on the adjustment disorder spectrum. The adjustment disorders may offer a more accurate explanation for the source of the child's symptomatic behavior and should be used as the basis for decisions about treatment.

The effect of the child's environment is always relevant even for those children who, in the absence of other stressors, meet the diagnostic criteria for ADHD. The ENIGMA study's finding that anomalies found in children's brains with attention deficit hyperactivity disorder are not proportionately represented in the adult brain is critical because it suggests that the brains of these children will eventually catch up. Furthermore, by medicating them, we may be essentially short-circuiting or masking positive qualities associated with high interest, motivation, passion, or curiosity.

Alison Gopnik is a leading psychologist and philosopher and the author of *The Philosophical Baby: What Children's Minds Tell Us About Truth, Love, and*

The Meaning of Life (2004). She has done extensive psychological research with babies, and on pages 12 and 13, discusses the potential advantage of prefrontal immaturity in the brain.

> The prefrontal cortex is one of the last parts of the brain to mature…The wiring of this part of the cortex, the process of pruning out some connections and strengthening others, may not be complete until the mid-twenties… (It) is especially involved in 'inhibition'…It actually helps shut down other parts of the brain, limiting and focusing experience, action, and thought. But…inhibition has a downside if you are primarily interested in imagination and learning. To be imaginative, you want to consider as many possibilities as you can, even wild and unprecedented ones...In learning, you want to remain open to anything that may turn out to be the truth…The lack of strong prefrontal control may actually be a benefit of childhood. (p.12,13)

Our son's experience in elementary school was not unlike many third-grade boys. Had I or the teacher completed a diagnostic standardized checklist of symptoms, he easily would have met the criteria for attention deficit hyperactivity disorder, and although medicating him may have resulted in his increased conformity to the demands of that particular classroom, I was concerned that his positive qualities of curiosity, drive, and self-determination may be stifled. His brain had never been studied, but, even assuming that it had, and that he had been discovered to have a brain structure consistent with ADHD, the benefit of his fourth grade classroom proved to provide the opportunities he needed of increased flexibility, high-interest activities, and a collaborative relationship which ultimately promoted his self-reflection and personal growth.

Admittedly, there is an inconvenient friction between the individual needs of children who present with issues relating to attention or hyperactivity and the typical demands of a conventional classroom. However, before we start placing children's brains under an MRI machine, perhaps we should be paying more attention to the inherent possibilities that exist relative to the connection between interest and attention. I believe that this is at the center of the issue itself and the key to understanding the best way forward. Attention differentiated development is a reformulation of the diagnosis (ADHD) that is consistent with the scientific findings that children with these symptoms will eventually catch up. It also suggests an approach that respects who these children are and what they need rather than labeling them with a disorder.

When children are engaged in high-interest activities, other symptoms normally associated with ADHD, such as hyperactivity, disorganization, and losing or forgetting things, are likely to diminish or disappear. This was detailed in the results of a survey that was conducted with parents who had decided to home-school their children; these children had been diagnosed with

ADHD and medicated. According to the results, in the great majority of cases, the children were taken off of the drugs and had no particular problems learning under the conditions of home schooling.

> When they could pursue their own interest rather than paths laid out for them by others, and when they could play to their hearts' content, most had no trouble learning and no need for psychoactive drugs. (Gray, 2013 p.82-83)

By the time our son graduated from elementary school, my sense was that we had dodged a bullet. Our increased awareness of our son's *style* in the world contributed to our skepticism about how these attributes would translate, either favorably or unfavorably, in the middle school setting. On the one hand, we hoped that the increased freedom of changing classes, choosing from an array of extracurricular activities, and increased personal responsibility would appeal to his demonstrated need for autonomy. However, we also knew that there would be demands to complete increasing numbers of assignments and attend classes that held little interest for him. We would no longer have input regarding who his teacher(s) would be nor could we expect that middle school teachers would have the time to get to know our child in the way that at least some of his elementary school teachers had. It was difficult to predict what might happen in this new environment, and since we realized that his tendency toward nonconformity had nearly earned him one common childhood diagnosis, we were concerned that there may be a renewed effort to diagnose or medicate, particularly if he was unable or unwilling to conform to the school's expectations.

CHAPTER 4

The Middle Years

"People with great passions, people who accomplish
great deeds, people who possess strong feelings, even
people with great minds and a strong personality, rarely
come out of good little boys and girls." – Leo Vygotsky

I still remember the day a stranger came into my
house and somehow knew my name was mom. My back
had been turned away from the door to the room. How
could a voice descend two octaves overnight? I asked
him to repeat himself just so I could be sure that the voice
I had heard was his. When I taught middle school in the
early 1990's, it was like taking a master class in
developmental milestones to witness the variety of
shapes, sizes, and levels of maturity that entered my room
each day. I taught music appreciation which meant that
every student in the school came to my classroom once
per week. There were a few with obvious facial hair,
some who towered over me, and many unfortunate ones
who had to endure teasing (usually by the ones with
facial hair) because their voices still had not changed.

If you consider physical transitions alone, it
becomes clear why *middle* is a useful name for this stage
of schooling. I remember feeling that I had to be
something of a chameleon in my interactions with each of

the students given the infinite ways in which they presented themselves. The impact of developmental tasks related to issues of identity, belonging, and peer pressure was obvious. I witnessed those who were excited and felt proud about the prospect of having a homeroom, changing classes, and having study periods as well as the ones who were intimidated by this new opportunity for flexibility and some degree of autonomy.

By now, it had become clear that there were certain variables in our second son's environment that would likely continue to be essential predictors of whether or not his experience would be favorable. I was both optimistic and somewhat anxious about the increased numbers of people and situations he would be dealing with. In retrospect, I should have been able to foresee what was coming. It is not a quantum leap to move from, 'I want to do this instead' to, 'I don't believe I need to do this because it's a waste of my time, it's redundant, or I already know it.' He began honing in on the things he liked to do and that he was good at, and preparing oral arguments for why he shouldn't have to do the things he didn't like to do or thought were unnecessary.

The issues that resurfaced in middle school did not become problematic until his 7th grade year. He continued to engage in the things that had high interest for him, such as his increasing focus on music, but adamantly refused to do the things that he felt were unnecessary. This was a gradually developing source of contention with his teachers that was compounded by the fact that he could continue to test very well, whether or not he did his homework. His grades dropped, not because he didn't know the material, but because he failed to consistently turn in homework and other writing assignments. He excelled in mathematics and science despite the struggles relating to homework. His teachers would bemoan his lack of effort, but since he was able to learn the material and demonstrate that he had learned it, he simply could not understand what all the fuss was about.

Of course, as parents, we continued to urge him to do the things that his teachers were requiring, but often this is the time when parents find that they have to decide how much responsibility they are willing to assume for their child's school performance. And regardless of our encouragement, our son was unimpressed by the realization that if he didn't do certain things, his grades would decline; he simply wasn't motivated to achieve high marks if it meant he had to do things that he thought were unnecessary.

Complaints about his handwriting and work habits became more frequent. Not only was he impervious to the efforts of his teachers, but also much less influenced than most by peer pressure. Ironically, this proved to be somewhat of a silver lining in that it served to mitigate the results of future risk-taking behaviors. We had our share of the usual teenage capers in middle school, but more often than not, they were the product of his own ideas, and we felt fairly confident that his friends wouldn't be able to convince him to do something he didn't want to do any more than his teachers could.

I share this next little story only because I think we have to remember that we cannot expect teachers or schools to really know our children given the limited framework within which they must interact. By this time, our oldest son was being transported one day per week, with an aide, to the same middle school that his brother attended and the one that his sister would also attend the following year. This activity, which was part of the community outreach program within his facility, provided an opportunity for him to stay connected to his siblings and to his home community. He was able to be in the room with the stage band, of which his brother was a member, while they rehearsed. After his first visit, the band director telephoned me. I'm sure you can imagine my first thought. (What did he do now?)

However, the band director had actually called to express surprise that when our oldest son arrived to the room with his aide, his brother ran over to greet him by leaning into his wheelchair with an embrace, stroking his face, and speaking intimately to him. And reportedly, he did this seemingly oblivious to the other members of the stage band who were watching, which was even more surprising to the band director. Obviously, this was a very different call from the ones I usually received, and it was a relief given what I had anticipated might be coming.

Although our son's behavior was a surprise to the band director, and likely to the members of the stage band, it did not surprise me in the least. This was not just a reflection of our son's relative disregard for the opinions of the other students; he and his sister continued to have a strong bond with their brother. They were used to having him included, and because they had gradually grown to understand the unusual nature of his special needs, they did not have the same inhibitions relative to his limitations that their friends may have felt. The personal attributes and qualities children possess, some of which would likely impress any adult favorably, may not find expression in a typical school setting. Our son displayed gestures that were sweet, affectionate, kind, and truly responsive to his brother, as did his sister. He found ways to draw him out and communicate with him, and this quality was not limited to his brother; he exhibited the same sensitivity with younger nieces, nephews, and other young children he encountered.

It can be difficult to know for certain what the impact is on the development of the siblings of a profoundly disabled child, particularly when they have proven to be so different from each other. We watched both of our able-bodied children care for and love their brother. Our daughter recorded books on tape so that he could listen to them in the evening; our son prepared mix tapes of some of his favorite music. He was their brother, plain and simple; and they became desensitized to the fact that he looked different, was unable to walk or talk, and had random seizures that occasionally caused him to smile.

Our family had adapted to a difficult reality; each of us processed our feelings, developed attitudes, and made adjustments in ways that reflected our individual differences, a concept explored in a book by Helen Featherstone, *A Difference in the Family: Living with a Disabled Child* (1981). My husband and I both clearly loved him, but we stood in stark contrast to each other in our beliefs, our level of acceptance, and in our methods of dealing with the pain and sadness that was inherent in his critical health issues and profound limitations.

I was able to enjoy the limited things he could do; his smile and occasional laugh felt therapeutic for me, and, for the most part, I was able to set aside other feelings as I knew the day would come when we would not have him in our lives at all. I never responded well to someone pointing out that it must be sad for me or bittersweet. I was very busy and found that my advocacy for his welfare was the antidote to a situation which I could not control. He would smile when he heard our voices and when we put the dog on his lap in his wheelchair. Sometimes he made us laugh, and, in some inexplicable way, I felt he was a symbol of what had become our close and happy family.

The impact of this experience undoubtedly had a significant effect on our attitudes and decisions regarding our other two children. Not surprisingly, everything else fell into perspective. Ear infections, injuries, problems with friends, losing a game in sports, and yes, even refusing to do your homework because you think it's unnecessary took on a new meaning and a far less important one. This explains, at least in part, why the ongoing antics of our second son, which resulted in continued telephone calls from the school, did not become exaggerated in importance despite the fact that the reported transgressions were admittedly outrageous.

It was the kind of story that may have been of interest to Art Linkletter's, 'Kids Say the Darndest

Things' (1957), or Reader's Digest, 'Funniest True Family Stories' (https://www.rd.com/funny-stuff/funny-family-stories/) except for the fact that the words contained in our son's commentary could not be reprinted. On a particular school day, when evaluation slips intended to document the students' assessment of a substitute teacher were distributed to the class, our son offered his opinion of this particular *sub* (she happened to be a pretty young girl) by writing "nice ass" on the evaluation and signing his *friend's* name before he handed it in! Predictably, the teacher nor the principal found this amusing.

I still remember the discomfort in the principal's voice when he had to read aloud what my son had written. When I received such calls from the school, I found it difficult to assimilate what I was hearing. I never knew what was coming next; I only knew that I needed to be thinking quickly about how to respond. I found myself reassuring the principal that, of course, we would address this with him, and, at the same time, I was rendered speechless when he asked me why I thought he would do such a thing. Although I was sure that it was mostly fueled by his gregarious personality, a mischievous sense of humor, and a willingness to advance such a prank, I also knew that attempting to make such a case with the principal was not going to be well received.

Throughout middle school, there developed an

increasingly obvious discrepancy between our son's apparent academic potential and his performance. His reports from teachers at the middle school told the story of a child who could do very well in every subject and, in fact, did achieve high scores in most subject areas. Further, superior scores on statewide standardized tests confirmed that he was a very capable student. However, his increasing unwillingness to perform in the way that was expected of him compromised his opportunities as he moved from one grade to the next.

In spite of the fact that he had distinguished himself in math, he was told repeatedly that he had to show his work in order to demonstrate how he had arrived at the correct answer, and because he was unwilling to comply, his eighth grade math teacher was reluctant to recommend him for honors math at the high school. In his mind, if he could get the right answer without showing how he got there, why would he bother to write it down? He never could accept the concept of what he considered to be unnecessary or *busy* work.

In 2005, Deborah L. Ruf, Ph.D wrote a book, called *Losing Our Minds: Gifted Children Left Behind,* in which she describes the negative effects of having the same requirements for every student, regardless of their ability or their interest.

> Many boys become more and more angry about all of the things that they are expected to do in school…things that make no sense to them and

seem like a waste of time. (Some) refuse to turn
in assignments or compete their work. They are
then accused of being disorganized, not paying
attention, and underachieving…(it) keeps them
from (having) opportunities that might work for
them. (p. 245/270)

Notwithstanding our son's resistance to putting
forth effort in school, he was highly self-driven and
ambitious. The day that he turned fourteen years old, he
requested that I drive him to our local grocery store
where he secured the promise of a job; the job was
contingent on his having a work permit which he
acquired that afternoon at the town hall. We had not yet
mentioned the idea of work to him; in fact, he grew up in
a town where many of the students were privileged and
did not work after school. But, unlike much of what he
experienced in school, the idea of having a job was his
own, and, in his mind, having his own money would
allow him to feel more control over his life.

Upon our return from a rare weekend getaway, my
adult nephew and his wife, who had agreed to care for
our children, were found to be incredulous that, in our
absence, our son had requested that they drive him to
Sears so that he could buy a television set for our
bedroom. They were equally incredulous that, when it
came time to leave for the store, he adamantly refused to
wear a coat. These events clearly illustrate the central
paradox that, for him, pitted control against freedom and
became the paradigm that dictated his response to most

situations. When in control, he would exhibit extraordinary acts of generosity, helpfulness, and compassion; however, when not in control, he was likely to experience the situation as threatening to his need to make his own decisions irrespective of the degree of importance inherent in the conflict itself.

In the end, it was easy to understand why our son's powerful need to make his own decisions created concerns and challenges for some of his teachers, and it seemed incongruous that someone this bright simply could not go along with conventional demands in spite of his belief that they were not worthy of his time. These qualities of strong will and self-determination had not lessened from the time he was a little boy nor had anyone been able to convince him that his life would be better if he would simply do the things that people asked him to do. But everything he heard seemed to be filtered through his own examination of how important it was for him, and his answer to that question would dictate whether, and to what degree, he would comply.

Relative to our son's resistance to standard classroom expectations, I have asked myself whether there may have been a different outcome had his teachers allowed him to demonstrate his knowledge in the way that he was most able to. How difficult would it be to allow such a student to opt for an oral exam rather than a written one if this is more consistent with the way they are best able to communicate what they know? And yet, this type of accommodation is usually made only after someone has been labeled with a disability.

I have also wondered exactly how my son was able to come up with the correct mathematical answer in his head rather than on paper; as a teacher, I would think that it would be interesting to have him explain that process verbally rather than to spend time arguing with him about his unwillingness to write it down. Who knows? Maybe if someone had taken that approach with him, he may have wanted to *try* to write it down for the benefit of the other students. Instead, they focused on his failure to comply. And simply because children don't learn in the same way as other students and/or possess more skill in verbally communicating than in writing, these are not, nor should they be, insurmountable obstacles to their progress. Unfortunately, the increasing struggle over whether he would comply with teacher's demands ultimately dominated his experience at the middle school, only serving to create further disengagement from the school's agenda.

In spite of this growing tension, he seemed happy with his life. He had friends, enjoyed playing in the band and didn't seem to mind that he wasn't getting straight A's as long as it was his decision to make. He continued to engage in the extracurricular things that interested him, including sports and music. Although his teachers were unhappy with him, he was not unhappy with himself. And since he basically dismissed their concerns and was increasingly unmotivated to perform in the way that they were insisting he perform, my sense was that his pranks, at least in part, reflected his attempt to make his middle school experience more meaningful and to alleviate his growing boredom.

As parents, we found that letting him make many of his own decisions had not been a problem. We recognized that, in addition to his being strong-willed, he was also responsible, funny, generous, compassionate, and driven to succeed. And in our minds, the dilemma we faced was increasingly centered on how the expression of these attributes could be enhanced by his qualities of drive and self-determination rather than stifled by them. Unfortunately, the inherent tension between continued demands for conformity, and the effective reconciliation with these seemingly contradictory traits, would only intensify in high school, ultimately resulting in crisis.

CHAPTER 5

ODD

An <u>O</u>verwhelming <u>D</u>etermination to <u>D</u>ecide

"The voyage of the best ship is a zigzag line of a hundred tacks." – Ralph Waldo Emerson

Playing high school football helped, but it would not be enough to avoid the looming crisis. Our son's unwavering determination to do the things he was interested in resulted in ongoing, increasingly vocal disagreements with teachers. He was totally committed to the idea that he needed more time to devote to music, an endeavor that had become increasingly important to him, and, in his mind, the school was interfering with his personal goals. He spent a great deal of energy attempting to defend this position; as a result, predictable struggles with his teachers became more intense and acrimonious. He was unbridled in his open refusal to comply; for him, there was no such thing as backing down.

By now, a damaging and toxic process had begun to set in; his growing frustration with the school's attempts to force him to conform, and his feeling of being trapped in what he experienced to be an intolerable situation, would result in increasingly high-risk behaviors. Our son's propensity to use his verbal skills to promote his position was no longer limited to the school; when he was returned home in the back of a police car after having been caught smoking marijuana with his friends in the town center, he challenged the officer about the relative importance of spending police time trying to chase down high school kids. Needless to say, the officer was surprised that he was not more contrite, and in an unexpected gesture of adult wisdom and compassion, he reflected, "I was sixteen once too."

These seldom offered expressions of understanding by other adults in our son's life were welcome and often surprising support; during this difficult stage of his and our journey(s), a particularly thoughtful and perceptive commentary was documented in an evaluation by the assistant principal during his sophomore year. "There are reasons for his frustration and provocative behavior that are not central to his basic nature. He is a very articulate, thoughtful and considerate person when not on the defensive." However, as comforting as some adults could be, they were not able to reduce our increasing concern about how much higher the stakes had become, and we feared that the escalation of risky behavior could have serious and potentially permanent consequences. By now, we had discovered that he was growing marijuana in his bedroom. He seemed increasingly unhappy, sullen, and disengaged. He would not hesitate to simply get up and walk out of any given classroom while announcing to anyone who would listen that they were wasting his time. He was suspended for drinking alcohol at school. As well, he occasionally found himself in court with misdemeanor related offenses along with his friends.

It can be a seamless journey from one diagnosis to another; roughly 50% of children and adolescents with ADHD are also diagnosed with oppositional defiant disorder (Matthys & Lochman, 2010). It would be difficult to argue that our son was not being oppositional or defiant at school, and his growing unhappiness was now also causing him to replicate those same behaviors in the community with law enforcement. Predictably, the transition of these difficulties from school into the broader community resulted in increased tension in our relationship with him as well. At the same time, however, he continued to work outside of school, assuming jobs with increasing responsibility.

Oppositional defiant disorder, like ADHD, is one of the disruptive behavior disorders in the *Diagnostic and Statistical Manual of Mental Disorders* (5th ed. DSM-5; American Psychiatric Association, 2013), and, in order to meet the diagnostic criteria, a child or adolescent must display a pattern of negativistic, hostile, and defiant behavior lasting at least 6 months, and exhibiting at least four of the following symptoms:

- Often loses temper
- Often argues with adults

- Often defies or refuses to comply with adults' requests or rules
- Often deliberately annoys people
- Often blames others for his or her mistakes or misbehavior
- Is often touchy or easily annoyed by others
- Is often angry and resentful
- Is often spiteful or vindictive

In addition, the following qualifiers must be met:

- The behavior must occur more frequently than is typically observed in individuals of comparable age and developmental level.
- The disturbance in behavior causes clinically significant impairment in social, academic, or occupational functioning.
- The behaviors do not occur exclusively during the course of a psychotic or mood disorder.
- Criteria are not met for conduct disorder, and, if over 18 years of age, criteria are not met for antisocial personality disorder.

Our son's attributes of willfulness and self-determination defined the challenges he experienced throughout his life, first at home, then almost entirely in the school environment, and, finally, in the larger community. His determination to decide things for himself was a strong constitutional trait that never changed; he was unable to relinquish his self-determination to those who supposedly knew better than he did about what he needed for himself. I've often wondered if he would have more easily adjusted to a less developed culture where children had to stop school in order to work and help the family. When he did leave classrooms, and assuming he was granted permission, he would happily wash tables in the cafeteria. Seemingly, he found this much easier to tolerate than the boredom he experienced at having to sit through lectures or discussions that did not interest him or that he felt were interfering with his ability to achieve his goals.

I knew we had reached a critical turning point when I received a phone call one day from the principal: "Mrs. Russell, I don't know where to begin." She sounded desperate, told me that our son was standing outside of the building and that if we were unable to bring him home, she would probably have to call the police because legally he had to be in school. It had been yet another very bad day, and I believe there was a collective sense that something would have to change. The school recommended a full neuropsychological battery of tests to see if they could better understand our son's lack of compliance with the school's agenda.

The test results demonstrated that he was an exceptionally bright adolescent who had a significant difference between the verbal and performance domains of his IQ, a difference represented in only 2% of the population. It demonstrated that he had an extremely high verbal IQ and an average performance IQ. In subtests, weaknesses consistent with this profile were noted in areas such as the ability to sequence, organize, and integrate visual information. However, it was also clear from his testing that he was scoring at the 12th grade level on the Woodcock-Johnson Achievement Test (Schrank, Mather, & McGrew, 2014).

The school proposed that this differential between the verbal and performance domains of his IQ explained why he was refusing to comply with the school's expectations. They felt that it was too difficult for him to do the work, not that he simply was disinterested or refused to comply. However, studies relating to the reliability of IQ differentials in predicting educational outcomes have been shown to have unconvincing results and, as well, to over-identify those children with high IQs and average achievement (Clikeman, 2005). And, more importantly, the school's formulation of what was at the root of our son's difficulties in school could not be reconciled with our experience of our son.

Underlying his resistant and provocative behavior, there was a serious and self-determined adolescent who was impatient with what he perceived to be arbitrary obstacles that were preventing him from achieving his own goals. His behavior in school was inconsistent with the responsible, hard-working adolescent that he had proven to be outside of school. In our minds, he possessed both the aptitude and determination to succeed in the things that were important to him; in his mind, school had become irrelevant. He was eager to begin working more exclusively on his chosen area of interest and seemingly took refuge in often menial, part-time jobs where earning money supported his need for real-world responsibility and self-determination.

The school's recommendation was that he should attend a remedial school for students with non-verbal learning disabilities as well as emotional and behavioral challenges. By this time, our son was angry and depressed. There was no question in my mind that his emotional state would only worsen if he was placed in an environment against his will, where the staff would be taking the same approach that the school did, and one in which he would be forced to learn certain things in a certain way in order to remedy supposed deficiencies.

The decision we were now faced with seemed critical, and we were far less concerned about the school's suggestion that he would benefit from a remedial program so that he could improve his academic profile than we were about his emotional health. We felt that his growing unhappiness and risk-taking behaviors resulted from his feeling beaten down and misunderstood, and we knew something had to change. As a result, we sought further consultation from the same psychologist who had provided input when our son was only seven years old. He did not seem surprised by the direction our son's journey had taken. After reviewing the results of his neuropsychological evaluation, he met with our son individually and subsequently with us. His opinion was that sending our son to a remedial program, such as the one the school was recommending, would be detrimental. He shared our concern that academics, at this point, were not the issue. He felt that we should seek an environment that was better suited to our son's makeup and constitution, one that would provide an opportunity for him to heal and to refocus his energy on the things that he wanted to learn. He suggested that we visit the Sudbury Valley School in Framingham, Massachusetts, which I will say more about in the next chapter.

While reflecting on our son's journey, it became clear that the early signs of willfulness that appeared at home, and to a lesser extent school, eventually became focused almost entirely on the school setting. The approach we had adopted at home helped to alleviate the challenges he presented in the early years. Flexibility within the elementary school classroom, as well as the autonomy afforded by the natural process of matriculating to advancing grades, helped in later years, but it was not enough to avoid the inevitable crisis in high school. Our son's unhappiness, which was reflected in resistance, defiance, and risk-taking, was exacerbated by a school system with a rigid structure and prescribed goals. By its very nature, it did not represent the needs of adolescents who had individualistic tendencies; there are countless students who struggle with pressure to conform to school standards and who may manifest their feelings of frustration in other ways as well such as quiet underachievement, disengagement from the social community, or more serious self-destructive behaviors.

The development of standardized education, since the time of the Industrial Revolution, has effectively replaced opportunities and/or the need for children and adolescents to participate in responsible work for the benefit of family or society. This development frustrates adolescents who embrace independence and responsibility, and, at the same time, it deprives less self-driven students of the growth opportunities they may need to master the developmental tasks associated with gaining maturity. School systems that are highly competitive and that tend to reinforce singularly-focused traditional notions of success may be particularly frustrating for many students, especially those with commendable or uncertain goals which are contrary to the goals set by the adults in their lives.

A New York Times article provided troubling statistics that showed rising rates of depression and anxiety among students in the highly regarded and competitive school system in Lexington, Massachusetts (Spencer 2017). In this article, it was reported that students felt pressure from parents and the school to excel academically. Some parents believed that their child's academic accomplishments would contribute to his or her chances of success in life; at the same time, schools were influenced by statewide ratings which were determined, at least in part, by the percentage of their student body who received college acceptances, particularly to prestigious universities. And, in fact, Lexington High School was able to boast not only a high number of ivy league school admissions but also numerous recognitions of academic distinctions in statewide competitions.

In the same article, the results of a 2015 National Health Survey demonstrated that 95% of Lexington High School students reported being heavily stressed over their classes, and 15% said they had considered killing themselves in the past year. Subsequently, efforts by the school community to ease the effects of stress were reflected in the development of courses such as positive psychology, the pursuit of happiness, as well as activities such as laughter yoga and relaxation. Although the school's attempts to meet the needs of students was commendable, it is noteworthy that they felt compelled to create classes designed specifically to mitigate the detrimental effects of the school environment itself. This represents a sad and troubling commentary on the issue of priorities in education. Inflexible goals, which are determined by the systems in which adolescents find themselves, deprive them of the natural process of self-discovery as well as opportunities to realize their positive attributes in other ways.

In the real world, outside of school, diversity in personality as well as in knowledge is valued. Part of the task of growing up is to find niches that best fit one's personality. In the modern school classroom however, there is only one niche, and those whose personalities don't fit are seen as failures, or as suffering from a 'mental disorder' (Gray, 2013), p. 81

We need to look beyond testing, diagnoses, and college admission to understand how to better support adolescents. Most parents would say that they want their child to exhibit the motivation to achieve, but how can any individual feel motivated toward a goal that is not theirs? If we can pay attention to what we can see excites or interests our child, and if we can find a way to make certain that the child can pursue those interests in an environment that feels supportive, they likely will be able to harness the motivation they need to succeed.

When I shared our son's test results with him and later found them on my desk with the word "BULLSHIT" scribbled across the front in his signature handwriting, I knew that no one would be able to convince him that there was any reason he could not succeed in school if he wanted to, and, furthermore, the school's proposal that it was much easier to 'tell what he knows' as opposed to 'show what he knows' did not alter his belief about what he felt was at the root of his lack of cooperation with the school's requirements.

My proposed reformulation of opposition defiant disorder to an overwhelming determination to decide provides an alternative view that I believe more accurately reflects the temperamental vulnerabilities that drive the behavior of many children and adolescents who present with opposition or defiance. Moreover, in a more general way, it underscores the natural developmental journey of *most* adolescents who feel ready to be making at least some of their own decisions. This reformulation also provides parents and professionals with an empathic and productive pathway for tailoring their responses to what they perceive to be provocative statements and behaviors. The words oppositional and defiant center around the perceptions of the adult, who, in response to the offending youngster, feels compelled to level their authority in order to maintain control. By contrast, the words overwhelming, determination, and decide are about the child or adolescent and what he or she is experiencing. This is likely to foster a more productive and understanding response from the adult, one which may result in the consideration of a broader range of solutions to the conflict.

Children and adolescents who do not share these temperamental vulnerabilities, but who also present with symptoms consistent with oppositional defiant disorder, may well be responding to unfavorable conditions in their environment: family dysfunction, issues of abuse, neglect, or child abandonment. In these cases, an adjustment disorder diagnosis is a more accurate reflection of the youngster's struggle, and, therefore, their unresolved feelings should be processed and supported by a competent child or adolescent therapist.

Whether the child or adolescent's difficulties are rooted in issues of temperament or other environmental or psychosocial stressors, it is a misrepresentation of the child's struggle to focus primarily on the outward symptoms of oppositional or defiant behavior without searching for the underlying source. In the case of our son, the focus was on what he refused to do rather than on his drive and determination to succeed. His attempts to realize his own interests and goals could not be reconciled with the school's protocols which included maintaining the status quo of school authority and standardized expectations. We looked forward to our visit to the Sudbury Valley School with a guarded sense of relief and hopefulness.

CHAPTER 6
A Leap of Faith

'The Truest Wisdom is a Resolute Determination."
Napoleon Bonaparte

"I think we have a winner", were the words uttered by our son during his initial interview at the Sudbury Valley School in Framingham after he had learned that the students in this school determined for themselves how they spent the five hours that they were required to be there each day. It was a rare, positive, and encouraging expression about *anything* having to do with school as our son had come to feel beaten down and desperately unhappy about the developments in his home school. On the other hand, it was a source of tremendous anxiety for my husband when, in the same meeting, he was informed that there was no standard curriculum, and the students did not attend any formal classes unless they specifically requested them.

As we toured the large and inviting estate, there were children and adolescents strewn throughout the building and the grounds doing many different things; yet, the feeling was not chaotic. In fact, the students seemed to be engaging in activities with a sense of purpose and joy. The music area was of particular interest to our son, and we left imagining that he would spend the majority of his time during his visiting week (a requirement for all prospective students) in that building.

There are important philosophical disagreements about what it means to be an educated person. Is it someone who is able to remember many of the facts they learned in school in the areas of history, science, and mathematics, or is it someone who has learned how to research and critically think about the things that they are truly interested in? Admittedly, there are many students for whom a conventional school environment is consistent with their learning style and therefore effective in educating them in a way that meets their understanding of what it means to be an educated person. Likewise, there are fields of study that these individuals are likely to embark upon that rely quite heavily on retaining facts and that emphasize a linear path for learning, which is dependent on the mastery of increasingly challenging material.

But there are many students, myself included, for

whom facts are meaningless unless they are connected to an area of high interest or have some practical use. A good example is that I do not remember many of the basic facts that I learned in classes such as American history or mathematics. However, in my job, I oversaw multiple contracts that provided children's mental health services. Each of these contracts had designated and seemingly random numbers that I remembered without difficulty and could retrieve when necessary. Likewise, I became proficient in computing percentages and analyzing data in order to assess staff productivity and/or program viability, in large part because I was passionate about the work I was doing.

Daniel Greenberg, who founded the Sudbury Valley School in Framingham, Massachusetts in 1968, received a PhD in theoretical physics from Columbia University and subsequently served on the faculty, both in physics and history. His passion for education is expressed in the innovative school he created and in the numerous books and articles he has written.

> There is a huge fallacy underlying our educational system today. That fallacy, briefly, is that everybody should know something about everything…we live in a culture with a vast array of specializations, by people who focus on particular skills and use them with a high degree of expertise…what we look for in any individual today is precisely the ability to execute, competently, the job they have undertaken, on which the rest of us depend. When we go to a

doctor's office, we don't care whether s/he is well versed in Shakespeare, or has a solid acquaintance with American history. In short, what makes for a person's success in our eyes is excellent knowledge and performance in their chosen field of endeavor (2001).

The Sudbury Valley School philosophy is embodied in three basic tenets: educational freedom, democratic governance, and personal responsibility. Students are not required to conform to an established curriculum; rather, they engage in the things that interest them. The underlying belief is that children are curious by nature, and that they will learn what they need to know in order to become responsible adults in society. Moreover, this occurs best within the context of a flexible environment, one that allows for frequent and spontaneous communication among students and staff. The school has remained committed to these principles despite predictable criticism, skepticism, and/or pressure to conform to institutional standards developed by the Department of Education and others. Here, students between the ages of four and eighteen look forward to returning each day to continue to work on the things that are important to them, whether it's practicing in the music rooms, painting in the art studio, reading, cooking, planning an event, or most importantly, playing and communicating with each other. There are no organized classes or formal instruction unless requested by an individual student or group of students, at which point one of the staff will provide it. Students are not separated into groups by the school; rather, children of all ages are free to mix as they wish. In this environment, the belief is that it is the social interactions between students and staff that best support a child's cognitive development.

It is difficult to avoid developing responsibility in such an environment, where you are called upon to think about and vote on all of the issues that impact your life and the lives of the larger community each day. For some students, like our son, this aspect of the school would be experienced as a welcome relief from the authoritarian framework of the public school he had attended; more reticent students, on the other hand, would discover the opportunity to develop confidence in having and expressing their own opinions. Regardless of where students are on the spectrum, such a system fosters the ability to consider issues that may require reconciliation of competing interests and to participate in the implementation of policies, laws, and rules that are required to exist in order for a self-governing democratic community to be successful.

In spite of these positive opportunities, however, our son's persistent and, as yet, unresolved issues with autonomy and authority would re-emerge; the lingering imprint of his experience in public school would threaten the freedom he had been seeking and demand resolution. The free and open democratic process of the Sudbury Valley School provided a non-threatening environment which allowed him to view his own behavior through the lens of a much wider community. Ultimately it was the weight of that collective body, of which he was a member, that enabled him to reconcile his need to make his own decisions with the necessary standards that must be created to ensure a successful self-governing community. Now, instead of the adults in his life telling him that he needed to change his behavior, it was the school community which included his peers.

In the Sudbury Valley School model, any student could ''bring up' another student at the weekly school meeting for the purposes of adjudicating perceived offenses. After several appearances before the committee designated to hear such charges, our son was suspended from the school for one week. Subsequently, he was afforded an opportunity to reappear before the same committee and to explain to them why he thought he should be re-admitted. His readmission was dependent upon a vote by the entire school body.

You can imagine that, as parents, this was an anxious time for us. We had taken what we felt to be an educated risk in sending our child to a school that basically supported and promoted our son's individualistic tendencies, and we worried about what would happen next if he was unsuccessful in this environment. It is difficult now to know where his life would have gone had he not finally reconciled his need for self-determination with the needs of the larger community. But what changed is that he had come to value his experience at the Sudbury Valley School, the people he encountered, and the respectful protocols that informed daily life. Since parents were not involved in the student's life at the school, we actually don't know what he said the day that he appeared before the school community to address their concerns; we only know that the vote was unanimous to readmit him.

The decision for our son to transfer to the Sudbury Valley School after his sophomore year was not an easy one, either for us or for him. Although he was very unhappy in the public school he had attended, he would be leaving good friends, some of whom he had been in school with for many years; and although we couldn't be sure we were making the right decision, our hope was that such an environment would alleviate the detrimental effects of his previous school experience. Gradually, our son's emotional wounds healed. The anger and frustration which had previously consumed him dissipated. He became happy with his life again, which consisted of days beginning early in the morning at a local country club, where he worked for several hours in the maintenance department, then driving to school so that he could continue to spend time on what he believed would be the direction of his life's work.

He relished the freedom to spend several hours a day in the music barn, communicating freely with other students and school staff while developing meaningful and productive relationships. He very quickly became well regarded in the music area, where he rehearsed with other interested students and assumed an active role in orchestrating the school's evening music shows. The staff experienced him to be a sensible, reliable, and hardworking student who brought positive energy to the music program and from whom other students began to rely on for help.

An interesting footnote relates to the earlier consultation we had received from the psychologist who had recommended that we visit the Sudbury Valley School during the time that our son was having so much difficulty in his home high school. At that meeting, he also mentioned the idea of military school. He felt that, because of our son's strong tendencies toward self-determination, these were the only two options that may work to successfully alter his path. He recommended that we start by visiting the Sudbury Valley School, but also acknowledged that many parents found this type of school to be a bridge too far in terms of the amount of perceived freedom; his experience was that these parents found more comfort in sending their child to a military school, a place where they could feel certain that their child would be forced to comply.

The inherent contradiction between a totally free school and a military school punctuates the central dilemma that parents in our position, and professionals, find themselves in. It was clear that our son could not be controlled in the conventional sense, although perhaps he could be forced to comply in the same way that Dr. Dobson forced his dog (Siggie) if it became necessary. However, knowing our son's determination not to back down, it was not a chance we were willing to take. Furthermore, it seems to me that a military school teaches a young person that someone else can force you to comply by using punitive, non-negotiable punishment. But that is not how the real world works when one leaves school nor is it a viable guidepost for dealing with life's challenges. The Sudbury Valley School focuses on the personal growth that will ultimately support and sustain whatever decisions the student makes about his or her own life. I feel confident that our son's personal development, which was reflected in a more mature understanding of the inherent challenge in reconciling issues of freedom and compliance, would not have been attained in a military school.

Currently, there are at least fifty schools that are based on the Sudbury school model throughout the United States and other countries, including Belgium, Japan, Denmark, France, Germany, Switzerland, Brazil, and Ireland; each is a separate entity with unique characteristics. Parents often wonder what happens to students who attend a school like Sudbury Valley. Will they go to college? Will they be able to get a job? Will they be able to compete with children who have attended only traditional public or private schools?

During 2002 and 2003, a study was completed of 119 graduates who had been enrolled at the school for at least three years and who left before 1998 in order to answer these and other questions relating to values, relationships, and happiness (Greenberg, Sadofsky, M. & Lempka, 2005). The respondents ranged in age from 21 to 49 years and attended the school sometime during the years between 1968 and 1998. Approximately half were male and half were female. Almost 50% were enrolled for six or more years, and approximately 24% were under the age of eight at enrollment.

The data shows that 82% of alumni pursued formal study after graduation, and 20% of those attended graduate school. The list of undergraduate and graduate schools they attended is long, varied, and includes a similar range of programs as one would find to be attributed to the general population. When respondents were asked why they chose one particular school over another, only 7% of respondents gave the reason that they were meeting external expectations; the most common reasons given were to pursue a specific career of their choosing, to gain deeper knowledge, or to satisfy the desire to be challenged. Graduates also were found to have embarked on a wide range of occupations, both traditional and non-traditional. The most frequently represented areas were in management, business, computer, education, arts, design, entertainment, and media.

Respondents to an earlier study of graduates noted that their attendance at SVS had benefited them for their future education and careers in several important ways: they had learned to be responsible and self-directed; they reported being highly motivated to learn more about, and to work or to find employment in their chosen careers; they reported that they had learned the skills and attained the knowledge necessary to continue to pursue their area of interest and, finally, they did not fear authority figures, which they attributed to the respectful relationships that they enjoyed with adults at the school, and to their experiences of articulating their views at sessions of the School Meeting and Judicial Committee (Gray & Chernoff, 1986).

Although our son was eligible to petition for graduation from the Sudbury Valley School after three years, he decided to remain for an additional year. He was engaged in a setting which he came to value not only for the opportunity it provided him to work on and learn the things that were important to him, but because he was in the process of deciding what he wanted to do next. Students are individuals with different degrees of readiness for any given transition in life; the Sudbury Valley School respects that difference and provides students with the time that they need to make those decisions for themselves.

There is only one requirement for graduation from the Sudbury Valley School, and it is the same for everyone: you must write a thesis advancing the proposition that you are ready to be a responsible adult in society and defend it before a committee chosen by the school community. Not surprisingly, our son's thesis included his recognition of the importance of reconciling issues of freedom with personal responsibility.

During his time at the Sudbury Valley School, our son's interest in music persisted, and, by the time he graduated, he had decided that he wanted to attend the Berklee College of Music in Boston. When we asked him if he thought he should apply to more than one college, he said that if he didn't get in the first time, he would just keep applying until he did. *And there you have it.* Although his ability to reflect on himself, and the world he needed to reckon with, had definitely changed, his basic nature had not. His singular, goal-driven energy had not lessened nor had his confidence in his ability to achieve the goals he set for himself. Fortunately, he had only to apply once and thereafter enjoyed four years studying music production and engineering, ultimately graduating with honors.

His success in qualifying for this particular major was dependent on achieving high marks, not only in subjects related to his area of specialty, but in subjects that are required in most standard accredited college curricula, such as English and history of civilization. These courses require a significant amount of reading, writing, and test-taking; and based on his successful performance, it is clear that the previously diagnosed non-verbal learning disability had little, if anything, to do with his failure to comply with his home school's requirements.

Our son is one of thousands of students who, for many reasons, feel disenfranchised from the schools they are attending, in large part due to the standardization of elements ranging from same-age clustering and rigid curriculum requirements to the decreased tolerance for students who detract from or question the goals of these institutions. I believe it was a sign of strength that our son held fast to his convictions about what he needed for himself, and it is far more concerning to me that countless other students find expression of their unhappiness in quieter, more self-destructive methods.

> Students in this country are thus becoming ever more rebellious, uncooperative, escapist, and desperate…No matter how many teachers (taskmasters) exist, no matter how small the classes, how many tests are administered…there appears no remedy. Even medicalizing the natural human processes of learning…introducing a plethora of 'illnesses' labeled 'disabilities', treating with special programs and medications, has produced little more than growing misery among the student population and growing dissatisfaction among teachers, administrators and parents (Greenberg, 2016), p. 29,30.

In hindsight, it would be difficult to argue that the Sudbury Valley School was not the right setting for our son, and it felt important that I reflect on exactly which elements and aspects of the school contributed positively to his experience. But after he graduated, I was left wondering about the larger lessons learned and how those same elements and aspects of this type of school serve to support any students' growth. It may seem counterintuitive to think that a school with no mandatory coursework can actually provide youngsters with *more* of what they can benefit from than the myriad of required classes, tests, standards, and *hoops to jump through* found in conventional settings. Perhaps it challenges all of us to think about exactly what it is that we want our children to learn.

CHAPTER 7

How and why Self-directed Education Works

"Tell me and I forget, teach me and I may remember, involve me and I learn." - Benjamin Franklin

For many people, when they discover something good, they want to share it; for me, that was the case with the Sudbury Valley School. Of course, it was gratifying for us to witness the transformation of our son from his despair into the young adult he was meant to be; and I would be less than truthful if I did not say that we felt somewhat vindicated by the developments in his life, both during his time at Sudbury Valley and after.

To that end, I shared the information about the Sudbury Valley School with a friend whose son was not *making it* in public school, and his experience would underscore for me one of the most valuable underlying tenets of Sudbury Valley. Unlike our son, this youngster was seemingly unmotivated to do anything, and according to reports by his mother, he spent his visiting week at the Sudbury Valley School sitting under a tree, eventually getting stung by a bee. This development was particularly troubling for his parents; they were hoping that their son would suddenly become motivated by the freedom that a school like Sudbury Valley offers.

But let's consider why this young man did not respond as his parents had hoped. The basic underlying philosophy of the Sudbury Valley School is that *all* children are born with the inner drive and curiosity to learn. In traditional school settings, disinterested students are often forced to sit and listen to their teachers, and, at the same time, are denied the opportunity to engage in the things that they *are* in fact motivated to learn or to do. It is reasonable to deduce that, over time, some children may lose their motivation to engage at all and may not be able to easily retrieve that motivation when such restrictions are lifted.

> "…most young people who enter our school have to go through a period of painful adjustment to freedom…(they) are rarely able to shake off all the effects of prior exposure to external control …they usually find it (harder) to develop internal feedback mechanisms to replace external controls…Those who adjust most easily are those who never went to another school…or who were ferociously rebellious in other schools and held their freedom more precious than anything." (Greenberg, 2016), p. 181.

The idea that we may be discouraging the very qualities that we want our children to develop is an important one. Most parents, when asked, would say that they want their children to grow up to be self-reliant, independent, and responsible. And yet, for many children, the development of these qualities may inadvertently be discouraged by the very conditions of the system in which they exist, one that effectively limits their exposure to opportunities that would allow for independent decision making.

At Sudbury Valley, our son's strong desire for self-determination was appreciated and nurtured by the staff rather than discouraged or disparaged. It was treated as an asset, which supported our son's motivation to achieve his own goals. He was accepted for the individual that he was and for the things he wanted to accomplish. There were no preconceived notions of what he should be like or what decisions he should make for himself. His individuality was embraced, and, not surprisingly, he developed mutually respectful relationships with staff that eventually broke down his resistance to hearing others' thoughts. Unlike most of his previous experiences, the adults in his life were no longer telling him that they knew better than he did about what he wanted or needed for himself.

By accepting him for who he was and encouraging him to pursue his own interests, the issue of authority ultimately became a non-issue because, in fact, the authority in a setting such as Sudbury Valley is not embedded in an hierarchical construction designed to delegate more power upon one person than another; rather, authority is realized through the collaborative relationships that staff members develop with students, the respectful and supportive tone of those relationships, and the collective aspect of the school community itself.

Naturally, I have wondered about other, seemingly more traditional and compliant children and how such a setting may impact their development. Recently, I discussed this issue with my daughter. We spoke about the freedom that is inherent in a school such as Sudbury valley and the lack of direction from authority figures; her insight was notable and worth repeating. She said that she thought that she had enjoyed the structure of public school and liked having received guidance and direction, but she wondered whether, if she had attended a school like Sudbury Valley from the beginning, she would have just naturally relied on herself to make decisions and to create whatever structure she needed for herself. She also wondered whether, now, making consequential decisions would be less anxiety producing had she had the freedom to make those decisions for herself throughout her lifetime.

We also spoke about the issue of self-discipline, and, in this instance, she questioned whether the requirements of doing homework and meeting certain academic requirements, even ones that didn't particularly interest her, helped prepare her to be successful in college and in law school. I thought about the connection between motivation and self-discipline, and how students who attend the Sudbury Valley School seem well able to harness the discipline they need to be successful when they decide that there is something specific that they want to accomplish. Whether those activities are things they do during their time at the school or things they do for a specific job or profession, they are able to draw upon their own desire and free will to regulate themselves to meet those challenges.

It is an interesting question about what drives the ability to accomplish one's goals. In the case of our daughter, she was motivated to attend and complete law school, and without the inner motivation to achieve this personal goal, it is difficult to imagine that she would have been able to sustain the level of concentrated study that is required to complete this process. Did reading and writing assignments in public school provide her with the opportunity to practice the demands she would face in law school? Maybe. Would the lack of those requirements have prevented her from being successful in completing law school? Our daughter was an avid reader; she had distinguished herself in the area of language arts, and she possessed strong reasoning and analytical skills. Given that we know that former students of the Sudbury Valley School have successfully completed graduate programs without the requirements of completing homework assignments, it is logical to deduce that our daughter would have been successful in achieving this goal as well.

This highlights one of the common and most profound differences between self-directed education and public school. In a school such as Sudbury Valley, it becomes the student's responsibility to achieve his or her own goals. They do not rely on someone else to assume that responsibility for them; and the development of responsibility in our children is something all parents concern themselves with. A common phrase we often hear is, *why can't you behave responsibly*? Haven't we all heard or said this at one time or another? But what experiences actually contribute to a child's development of personal responsibility? It may not be enough to require that our children perform the tasks that we assign them such as school homework or taking out the trash. If we expect our children to develop real personal responsibility, it may be of more benefit to them to provide opportunities to make and to debate real life decisions and to experience the consequences of those decisions, good or bad.

At Sudbury Valley, students and staff have an equal voice in the welfare of the collective community. All students are privy to most aspects of the school's operation, and they are invited to participate in all decisions that impact the school community. When an individual is genuinely responsible for his or her own environment and welfare, the idea of personal responsibility becomes real and is able to be practiced in a very real way. It is not some vague concept that your parents or teachers talk about, and it does not always develop as one might hope from a directive to accomplish designated weekly assignments or as a reprimand for some transgression of childhood.

Here, students can and do rely on themselves to shape and direct their own lives; their education becomes their responsibility, and their personal growth supports them in attaining their goals.

> I think that my confidence in myself, as well as my ability to tackle whatever it is that I want to tackle, in large part came from having been given the trust to shape my own education, and the trust that I would know what was best for myself from a young age. I have never found myself in a situation where I feel like I don't have the tools to tackle something, or the inner strength, direction, and ability to do whatever it is I want to do. Greenberg D., Sadofsky, M., Lempka, J., (2005), 319,320.

In traditional education, students are increasingly required to meet goals that are set for them by school administration in the service of promoting them to college. The responsible student, then, unwittingly enters into an unspoken contract with their school to perform all of the necessary tasks designed to achieve this goal. Somewhere along the way, the student internalizes this agenda so that their goal *also* becomes that of getting into the best college they can, when, in reality, it may not be the best college for them but, rather, the one that has the highest overall rating. And, as a result, this goal often becomes devoid of any real consideration about interests, desires, or what one truly finds enjoyable in life. If we are concerned that this may not lead to the outcomes we desire for our children, and we believe that personal growth is central to a student's success in life, we may want to consider alternatives.

Recently I revisited the Sudbury Valley School, and during my visit, three little girls came into the office, one in tears; predictable recriminations ensued among the girls while they attempted to plead their individual innocence. But here is what was different. The staff truly knew these three little girls because the atmosphere of open communication allowed for the development of that insight and resulted in a deeper understanding of each of their needs; and it was this reality that enabled the staff to assist them in exploring their own behavior, their empathy or lack thereof for each other, and ultimately what they would decide to do about it.

The girls were aware that they could make a formal complaint against each other, a complaint that would have been adjudicated at the school meeting, but by the time the intervention was finished, they were in the process of reflecting on their own behavior as it contributed to the conflict and had developed a greater appreciation for each other's point of view. Their ultimate decision not to make any formal complaint, but rather to think further about the issue, is just one example of the benefits of a free environment in which issues can be addressed in the moment. This contributes to a child's personal growth and developing sense of personal responsibility. Many teachers in traditional classrooms perform nothing short of miracles in their attempts to accomplish similar feats each day. However, because they must conform to a very different model, which places them at the head of the class, and must marshal the children through a host of prescribed activities and required coursework, they do not have the time to devote to developing such relationships.

At the time that we enrolled our son in the Sudbury Valley School, we felt that we were doing so primarily in response to his specific needs, but the basic tenets of self-directed education offer important ideas that can benefit all students. Many children are currently receiving mental health diagnoses because they are forced to conform to school settings in which they cannot thrive. Further, there is a disconnect between the agenda inherent in conventional education and the actual challenges of today's world. The pace of change has become almost frantic, and unrelenting. The idea that imbuing our children with a standard set of facts, in a standard array of subjects, may no longer be relevant.

CHAPTER 8

The Problem with Diagnosis: Changing the Conversation

They Become What You See

Rarely does a day go by that I do not hear the words *on the spectrum* or *ADD* bantered about in casual conversation: it happens at the park, at the grocery store, in dentist's offices, and just about anywhere else you can imagine. It has become a standard reference for any number of things: poor eye contact, high energy, disinterest, preferred solitude, or even a critical moment in which a child feels overwhelmed. It is as though diagnoses that were created only thirty-five years ago have now become household names, often misunderstood and erroneously applied.

As I have been writing this book and speaking with other parents about the subject, it seems that everyone has a story to tell about how they feel their child, or a child they know, was misunderstood or mislabeled. Recently, I heard from a grandparent who shared a story about his grandson's school experience. The school had recommended to the child's parent that he be assigned to a special classroom because he wasn't reading. Fortunately, the father knew that the child could and did read when it was something of interest, which, in this case, was fishing. He shared this knowledge about his son and advocated successfully for him to remain in the regular classroom. Not only was this child at risk for being labeled with a reading disorder, but he was also likely at risk for being diagnosed with ADD. His disinterest in this aspect of classroom activity may well have been interpreted as inattention, distraction, or inability to concentrate. The fact that he tended to be a quiet or compliant child would not have prevented this diagnosis as there exists more than one type of ADHD, and the inattentive type does not require that the child be hyperactive. In this case, the parent's observation and understanding of the child was critical in preventing an inaccurate diagnosis.

There are important distinctions between adult diagnosis and childhood diagnosis. Unlike many children, adults can verbally describe what they have been experiencing: they can communicate about the connection between their thoughts and feelings and the events in their lives; they can consider possible genetic predispositions to a particular set of symptoms; they can also explore many other conditions, attitudes, or desires that may be contributing to their current difficulties. A verbal report by an adult may include a litany of complaints: lack of appetite, lack of motivation, difficulty concentrating, and/or feelings of sadness. Often, they can also tell us when they started to feel this way, whether they have experienced unexplained weight loss, and whether there have been events in their lives that seem to have precipitated this decline. In the end, we likely are able to feel confident in considering a diagnosis of clinical depression.

During the time that I supervised a social work program in a local hospital, I visited an adult in the critical care unit along with one of the social work staff who had expressed concern about this patient's mental status. When I asked the patient if she could tell me where she was, she reported that she was in Friendly's Restaurant. Even with further questioning, she was unable to recognize the contradiction between the surroundings of her bed, which included heart monitors and other medical equipment, with the surroundings in a typical restaurant, and since medical studies had ruled out any other possible cause, one could safely deduce that this was a patient who was psychotic, not in touch with reality.

But let's think about how much more difficult it is to confirm a diagnosis of schizophrenia in a child, which, although rare, does exist. Many children engage in pretend play; they may have imaginary friends, and they may resort to fantasy to deal with their lives if they have been traumatized. Furthermore, fantasy can be a useful strategy to avoid communicating information that they don't feel safe to share. Simply put, there are many other ways in which a child may appear not to be in touch with reality but, in fact, may not have childhood schizophrenia.

Years ago, a preschool aged girl was brought into my office with reported complaints of hyperactivity and inattention. She was described as darting from one thing to another and not listening. During my first individual session with this child, she quickly made her way to the large two-level wooden playhouse which was equipped with furniture, accessories, and most importantly, miniature figures designed to invoke representative images of family members. At the outset, it appeared that her attention to her play with these figures, as well as her actions, had a somewhat compulsive quality. She would play silently, moving the figures around, occasionally simulating contact between family members. Over several sessions, the source of her anxiety was revealed when she enacted sexual encounters between a father figure and a child.

Although part of the story had been unearthed, important questions remained. Was this a re-enactment of actual contact that was occurring between herself and her father? Was it a reflection that she was witnessing some type of pornography? The answer to these questions would come later, but, certainly, one very important question had likely been answered, and given this child's struggles, it was surprising that she was not more symptomatic. This child's impulsive, inattentive behavior was most likely rooted in the troubling reality of her experience at home; and if we simply diagnosed this young girl with ADHD and placed her on a trial of medication, it may well have masked not only her symptomatic behavior, but the real cause of her difficulties. Sexual abuse is an extreme example; however, this critical investigative process, one that must occur with young children in order to understand their presenting symptoms, is often overlooked.

In a community mental health agency, our therapists often witnessed the sad and troubling realities of many of the children's lives we served. Our ability to do this work was buoyed by the opportunity to uncover child maltreatment and to set in motion protective interventions. As well, by educating and supporting the non-offending adults in their lives and by fostering an understanding of the child's symptoms, conditions were created that offered the child an opportunity for a corrective emotional experience. Of course, the aftermath of any kind of abuse is more complicated than that and requires ongoing comprehensive treatment, but it is a beginning. And when we conduct an appropriate assessment, we can feel confident that we are treating the actual problem rather than merely the presenting symptoms.

Some latency aged children, who had been mistreated at home or elsewhere, were able to communicate their concerns verbally, but usually only after they had developed a trusting relationship with the therapist. Some children were afraid to reveal the events of their home life; these unfortunate children were keenly aware that a parent was at risk for losing parental rights. Perhaps the parent was using drugs, suffered from mental illness, or was unable to provide basic necessities for their child.

At the same time, children from highly functioning and intact families can be suffering from feelings of anxiety and sadness as well; and the degree to which those feelings manifest in the child's behavior is not necessarily a reflection of the objective severity of the child's experience. *My* level of sensitivity to conflict, or to perceived instability in my environment is unique to me and does not necessarily predict anyone else's; the same is true for children.

Diagnosis is quick; it's easy. Finding out what is in a child's heart and mind is not; and once we do know what is in a child's heart and mind, are we not ethically responsible for addressing whatever that is? If we discover that there are influences in the child's life that are likely causing their symptoms, we should focus our priorities on addressing those issues. This may mean family therapy; it may mean therapy for the adults in the child's life or making adjustments in the child's environment. It may also mean working with the child's teacher to foster an understanding about what is causing the child's behavior or exploring modifications that could provide support.

As parents, we see our children in a variety of

situations; we know what tends to trigger their anxieties. We see what their strengths are and what they are capable of. Parents know these things, and their holistic understanding of their child should be an important consideration in assessment. However, rarely is a parent treated like an expert. Parents have come to believe that they don't know as much as the professionals. They feel that the professional *must* know more than they do, so they listen; they may not feel empowered to challenge the professional, even when they have an inner voice that is telling them otherwise.

The process of child assessment must be holistic as well. An evaluator's interview of a parent should include not only a report of the child's challenging behaviors but also the parent's observation of what his or her child is doing when they are happy and engaged. They should ask the parent to describe their child and resist the temptation to conjure up a diagnosis too quickly. Describing opens up possibilities well beyond what is found in a short list of diagnostic criteria; it allows us to see the positive aspects of a child's temperamental orientation and can result in a creative exploration of what works, as opposed to what's wrong.

Parents who are seeking help with their child's challenging behaviors should take notice of whether the evaluator they choose focuses exclusively on what's wrong as opposed to what works. The likelihood that a child will end up with a diagnosis, and/or on medication, is far greater when the emphasis is on what's wrong. Conversely, the power of focusing on what works not only allows us to harness the child's positive qualities in addressing their difficulties, but it can also impact how a parent views their child and, more importantly, how they respond to the struggle.

CHAPTER 9

Understanding the Critical Role of Temperament

"The apple doesn't fall far from the tree."
– Eastern origin (1839)

So, who was the tree? From whom did our son inherit these temperamental tendencies? They certainly weren't from me, or his father who was much more reserved and measured. Instead, our son is remarkably more like *my* father who demonstrated the same, often contradictory qualities that we witnessed in our son. He was a highly ambitious and successful businessman who rubbed shoulders with the likes of the CEO's of General Motors and Pepsi. But he could also be found on any given Sunday afternoon presiding over a large Italian family dinner which he had helped to prepare, punctuating the event with an enormous (intended to provoke) belch, accompanied by a verbal testament that he was now full and felt 'pleasantly delightful'. This outrageous gesture was inevitably followed by a predictable plea for civility and comportment by my far more controlled and retiring mother, but typically to no avail.

He was also, by his own account, always right and could be inflexible and controlling. His emotional and sometimes unexpected reactions to things were usually rooted in strong paternal feelings of protection or responsibility. At the same time, he was highly generous and compassionate. He went to great lengths to make sure all of his children had everything they wanted or needed and was a reliable and devoted caretaker. He seemed to feel personally responsible when anything that went wrong with any of us, regardless of the cause. I still remember seeing my bicycle, from which I fell numerous times, being hurled to the ground in anger by my father after badly injuring my knee; and likely all of my siblings remember the time he was reduced to tears when he dropped a beautiful crystal Christmas tree that my sister had brought him from France, breaking a small piece off of one of the branches.

A child doesn't get to choose his or her basic temperament any more than they can choose whether or not they are Italian or Irish. The difference in temperament between our son and his younger sister was stark and could be observed in a number of ways, the most obvious of which was related to flexibility and emotional reactivity. During their early years, things which our daughter would relatively easily transition to because she needed to redirect, or accommodate a previously scheduled activity, instead were likely to become unpleasant incidents for our son in which he became openly and emotionally resistant. This contrast between flexibility and resistance would persist throughout their lifetime and significantly impact their experiences, particularly in school.

As young adults, they often had similar ideas about how things should be different than they were, or about things that they each wanted to accomplish, but the manner in which they attempted to effect the changes they desired reflected their respective approaches to the world. As an example, while in high school, each of them discovered that they had little appetite for the emphasis of achievement aimed at the primary, often singular, goal of attaining college admission; they experienced this underlying directive for students to be dictated largely by the high school administration and, to a lesser degree, ambitious parents.

Our daughter had excelled academically throughout her tenure in public school; she was an outstanding student who had distinguished herself in language arts, particularly in creative writing and poetry. But it became clear over time that she found the competitive high school atmosphere, which pitted student against student and parent against parent, stifling and irrelevant. She seemed to long for something more meaningful and separate from her high school environment, a place in which learning had become secondary to the anxious pursuit of achievement. Her academic standing bolstered her credibility in an effort to articulate a proposal to the administration that she be granted permission to spend a semester providing medical and rehabilitative care to wounded animals in Maryland, which her father insensitively referred to as '*road-kill*.' The administration agreed, and arranged a plan that allowed her to maintain her schoolwork while she was away. This alternative experience, similar to other programs students often considered for their *gap year*, was discovered through The Center for Interim Programs, (interimprograms.com). Such programs allow students to access unique and meaningful opportunities; for our daughter, the wildlife sanctuary fulfilled her passion for animals as well as her strong sense of social justice, which had continued from the time she was a little girl.

She effectively replicated this strategy in her senior year in order to participate in an independently discovered program called the Audobon Expedition Institute, sponsored through Lesley College in Cambridge, Massachusetts, (www.getonthebus.org). This program allowed her to spend the final semester of her senior year traveling through the American Southwest in a custom-designed school bus while eating, studying, and sleeping outdoors. Each of these opportunities encouraged and supported her maturation and self-discovery in a way that would have been impossible in the traditional high school setting.

But what is most notable, as it relates to this conversation about temperament and our daughter's experience, is that she very methodically went about the business of convincing the high school that she could not only complete her academics in these alternative settings but that this would be a valid and productive learning experience for her. She focused on justifying her case by gathering the information, meeting with the administration, and making her pitch. This was, and is, our daughter's general approach to most things; there is no control button that gets pushed for her. It was not that she cared any less than our son did about wanting to be doing something different from what the high school was providing; rather, her approach to the world is different.

A noteworthy footnote to our daughter's journey is that there was absolutely no recognition afforded her at the formal high school graduation ceremony despite the fact that she completed all of her high school requirements while receiving sixteen credits from Lesley College. By contrast, there were numerous awards bestowed for students who met specific standards of achievement that had been set by the high school, an unfortunate reality that presents an interesting metaphor for the constricted lens through which children and adolescents are evaluated in traditional education.

In an article entitled, "What Is Temperament Now?" (Shiner, et al. 2012), the findings of four early prominent researchers are reviewed and compared with more recent findings that contribute to our most current understanding of the issues surrounding the role and development of temperament. The most recent studies suggest that "Temperament traits are early emerging basic dispositions in the domains of activity, affectivity, attention, and self-regulation, and these dispositions are the product of complex interactions among genetic, biological and environmental factors across time" (p. 2).

Essentially, what this means is that children are born with basic traits, and we can recognize these characteristics in children early on by their presenting disposition. For example, we may notice how physically and emotionally active or reactive they are, their level of flexibility, their attention to stimuli, and/or their ability to calm or soothe themselves. If you have more than one child, you may have noticed that they exhibited differences from each other in basic temperament from the time they were babies. In fact, it is not uncommon to hear parents reminisce about how different their children were from each other *from the very beginning*.

So, what happens when you have two very different children who seem to need very different things from the world in which they find themselves? 'Goodness of Fit' (1977) is a concept first developed by Stella Chess and Alexander Thomas and remains a vital element in the ongoing discussion and debate about the role of the environment in supporting individual temperament. This concept relates to the degree to which a child's basic temperamental tendencies are supported by, and/or compatible with, their environment. When there is a poor fit, it is less likely that the child will be successful in meeting the demands or expectations of that environment; in fact, this often leads to disruption or lack of engagement on the part of the child. And not surprisingly, this, in turn, can result in the child receiving a mental health diagnosis.

As adults, we know that we are going to fare better in certain environments than in others. In my professional life, my success and satisfaction were largely dependent upon the environment in which I worked; it was important for me that I experience flexibility, variety, and autonomy in my job. Most of us gravitate toward positions that support our personalities and, hopefully, result in personal fulfillment. But children must rely on the adults in their lives to recognize their individual needs and to respond appropriately, whether that means making minor modifications in a traditional classroom or finding an alternative setting.

Our son's story unfortunately is not unique. There are countless students being left behind despite the *No Child Left Behind* legislation, and not because they do not possess the attributes to be successful, but because the rigid standards and teaching methods that must be employed to support same age classrooms and conventional educational goals do not work for them. When medication becomes a consideration, at least one of the questions we need to be asking is whether or not that particular child's reported symptoms would be lessened or disappear entirely in a different environment.

In his book, *Free to Learn* (Gray, 2013), the author references a study he conducted with children who were being home-schooled after experiencing difficulties in their school classrooms; in almost every instance, the symptoms that the child was experiencing in school were not replicated at home. Further, there is a significant body of evidence that supports the importance of the interplay between the child and his or her environment, both at home and in school, Meaney, (2001) and Felitti et al (1998).

Animal and twin studies each confirmed that neural pathways in a child's brain can be impacted favorably or unfavorably, depending on the quality of those interactions. As well, Swanson et al. (2002) showed that behavioral aspects of attention deficit disorder could be traced to the presence of an uncommon gene, and that parenting children with this particular variation showed that there were temperamental characteristics dependent on the style of parenting they experienced, Sheese et al (2007). In her book entitled, *Becoming Who We Are* (Rothbart 2011), the author sums up this idea of the interplay between temperament and environment.

> At home, the child's natural temperamental tendencies dictate their reactions to stressful situations, as well as their ability to adjust and to cope with change. In turn, the parent's own temperamental attributes and style will impact their reaction to the child and vice versa, so that there is an interdependence that will either negatively or positively affect the child's developing personality (Rothbart 2011).

This is also true in the school environment where the teacher's response to the child's natural tendencies will either support the positive aspects of that child's behavior and personality development or have a negative impact. This further emphasizes the importance of a teacher's ability to recognize and respond appropriately to differences in children given that all children are not temperamentally prone to behaviors that are easily managed in the traditional classroom.

Parents who understand their child's temperament are more effective in adopting parenting strategies that will effectively support their development. When parents and their children have different styles of temperament, it can be more challenging to empathize with what your child is experiencing, but the danger in not doing so is that it can become a source of conflict in your relationship.

> When a parent makes demands of a quality or in a form that are incompatible with the child's characteristics and persists in these demands, parent and child can become adversaries instead of friends. The parent interprets the child's inability to comply as 'willful disobedience' or (alternatively)'lack of discipline.' *Know Your Child*. (Chess, S., and Thomas, A. 1987) p. 78.

In schools, there have been some successful attempts to integrate the consideration of temperament into the classroom, such as the INSIGHTS Intervention (McClowry, Snow, Tamis-LeMonda & Rodriguez, 2010)

which targeted urban, primary grade children, their
parents and teachers. The results demonstrated that
children enrolled in INSIGHTS showed a significant
reduction in disruptive behaviors at home and at school.
In this program, parents and teachers are given
information about temperament and encouraged to
support the temperamental individuality of their own, and
other children. They are also taught strategies for
preventing and dealing with the related behavioral
challenges.

Attempting to raise a child without understanding
their basic temperament is like trying to drive to a new
destination without an address or a map A parent's
ability to effectively advocate for their child depends on
the commitment of the professional community to
consider the issue of temperament in their assessment and
in their feedback provided to parents; and if parents are
unfamiliar with the significance of the connection
between temperament and environment, whether it relates
to parenting issues or to decisions regarding school, it is
incumbent upon the professional to guide parents
appropriately. I am not suggesting that temperament is
destiny, but it is an important determining influence; and
how we manage, appreciate, discourage, stifle, or support
the basic tendencies of any given child will play a major
role in their development and in the person they become.

Over time, I have often reflected on the approach
we took and the decisions we made about our middle

child. Some years ago when our son was in college, I asked him how he thought he would have fared if we had just been more strict and unequivocal in our approach, perhaps even resorting to force from time to time, similar to the method proposed by Dr. Dobson and his adventures with his dog, Siggie. His response was immediate and simple; "I'm pretty sure you would have found my face on a milk carton."

My dog, an Australian labradoodle named Bella, is now five years old. When I brought her home in May of 2015, I was provided with a manual, *Raising Your Australian Labradoodle,* by Suzanne Goodwin (2014), breeder at Berkshire Hills Labradoodles in Western Massachusetts. In the chapter entitled, *Understanding Your Puppy*, the first paragraph may just as well have been written about children, as opposed to dogs, and offers a useful example of the value in recognizing and responding to individual temperamental characteristics.

> Try to forget how you think a puppy SHOULD act and see who your puppy really is. The Australian labradoodle is a super aware and sensitive dog...so it is important not to overwhelm your puppy or expect him to be a different kind of puppy than he or she is. Just be tuned into what they need, whether it is more time to adjust to changes or a chance to get their energy out before playing with the kids. Each puppy has their own needs and style of doing things! (p. 9)

CHAPTER 10

In the End

"A Mind Is a Terrible Thing to Waste."
United Negro College Fund

If you are feeling lonely or isolated, get a dog; not only do they provide companionship, but they create connections. During the year 2015, not long after having moved to Cambridge, Massachusetts, my puppy and I facilitated new friendships through a daily morning ritual which found us at her favorite place (the dog park), which was a short walk from my house. Depending upon which of her friends showed up with which owners, discussions of a wide variety of things occurred: politics, career, home improvement, and, of course, our respective dogs.

Cambridge is a diverse community with a large population of students who pursue college and advanced degrees at an impressive number of local universities. Many of the young people I spoke with seemed confident and enthusiastic about their education and career choices; but I had also taken note of the ones who felt stressed or confused about whether they were on the path they want for themselves. The flexible nature of his PhD thesis allowed one such young man to immerse himself in photography, something he had grown to love; his affect was bright as he described his feeling of privilege to be able to engage with, and photograph families in order to capture each of their unique stories. During an encounter with him at the park, he shared that he was nearing the completion of his thesis and would soon need to resume his medical career. He expressed disappointment and was seemingly conflicted about the prospect of leaving something behind that had brought him so much pleasure and fulfillment. I wondered whether he felt trapped by a trajectory that had become so compelling that there seemed to be no way to change course, and I also wondered which factors most influenced his decision.

I'm sure you must be wondering what ultimately happened to our son. In retrospect, it shouldn't have surprised us that he decided to embark on a business career after college. Years earlier, this was the child who, when sent to his room for time out, offered to remain for an additional ten minutes if we gave him $10.00 and who later, as an adolescent, reassured us that he wasn't going to smoke the fruits of the cannabis plant we found in his bedroom; he was only going to sell it! You can only imagine how relieved we were.

Recently, he shared an audio-recorded interview which had been conducted by a Berklee College of Music staff member. The interviewer was researching outcomes of post-graduate students, and, in particular, those who had matriculated into careers other than music. In it, our son spoke about factors of family precedence that influenced his decision to pursue an MBA; his cousins, uncle and grandfather(s) were all involved in pursuing business careers. He spoke about the autonomy and flexibility of his current job and about the similarities he was able to draw between creating music and developing a business proposal, both of which involve a skill set that he described as 'the ability to organize ambiguity by applying logic to things that are illogical.'

As I listened to the interview, I was struck by his confidence in the choices he had made, his ability to appreciate how each of those choices had influenced and supported the next one, and how he had learned to glean from each opportunity an understanding of the positive and relevant things he had learned. Most importantly, he seemed happy with his life and the decisions that he had made. I also thought about his journey, and the critical places where he may have lost his bearings altogether. I thought about how close we came to losing him to a different, much less rewarding life and how desperately unhappy he had become in the traditional school setting. I thought about the diagnoses he likely would have been labeled with had we not questioned the school's assessment or declined to give him the medications he may still be taking. And, of course, I thought about the strengths my son always possessed, and how those strengths were at the cornerstone of his progress and success.

Labels do matter; legitimate concerns exist about

stigma and whether a diagnosis will have an enduring impact on a child's life. But more importantly, inherent within the label of a childhood diagnosis is an implied formulation that suggests a recommended approach to treatment. By substituting the words differentiated and development for deficit and disorder in attention deficit hyperactivity disorder, it challenges teachers to consider modifications in the child's environment rather than to remediate and/or medicate a perceived deficit that will likely resolve as the child matures. Likewise, when we use the words overwhelming and determination instead of oppositional and defiant in oppositional defiant disorder, the conversation naturally shifts away from the adult's need to exact authority upon their child. Instead, the goal becomes to support the child or adolescent's determination to impact the decisions that are made about themselves, and, at the same time, it offers an opportunity to explore alternative solutions.

Changing how we think about the issue of child and adolescent diagnosis and treatment may also be informed by considering cultural differences among countries. During 2017, In France, less than .5 percent of school-aged children had been diagnosed or medicated for attention deficit hyperactivity disorder; in the United States, where that percentage was 11-14% for the same time period, there was, and continues to be, an emphasis on biology and brain studies which often results in diagnosis and treatment with medicine. By contrast, the

French believe that psycho-social and situational causes are at the root of children's behavior; therefore, treatment strategies naturally focus on the context of the child's environment as it relates to home, school, and/or community, (Wedge, 2012).

In the Netherlands, where the philosophy is that achievement doesn't necessarily lead to happiness, but rather that success *starts* with happiness, play is valued more than quiet obedience. Discipline, rather than being punishment-based, is about teaching socially appropriate behavior. Parenting is authoritative, not authoritarian; when a child puts forth an argument, it is not discouraged but rather seen as a useful life skill. In a 2013 UNICEF report, which rated Dutch children the happiest in the world, the United States ranked 26th, just above Lithuania, Latvia, and Romania, the three poorest countries in the survey. The importance of happiness for our children cannot be overstated; studies clearly demonstrate that happiness contributes to the development of self-confident, socially responsible adolescents, an empirically demonstrated fact which is illustrated by statistics that show very low rates of binge drinking and teenage pregnancy in the Netherlands (Acosta & Hutchinson, 2017).

When parents are challenged by a child or adolescent's behavior, they deserve to be connected to the appropriate resource. Well trained child and adolescent specialists in the fields of psychology, psychiatry, and social work, as well as developmental-behavioral pediatricians should have a primary voice in the diagnosis and treatment of children and adolescents. However, the professionals who are best equipped to explore the child's inner experience, and to understand and identify the source of the child's difficulties, are often sidelined in the service of a quicker, easier, and more simplistic assessment.

An impressive body of knowledge exists which reflects contributions from many sources in the professional community, but it is not always well coordinated. Mental health professionals may be familiar with the nuances of differing skill sets, but parents may not, nor should they be expected to. Therefore, it is incumbent upon those who are making referrals for child or adolescent evaluations to make certain that they understand the unique aspect of child/adolescent assessments and to provide the parent with appropriate options.

I was privileged to oversee the assessment and treatment of children and adolescents in a large mental health clinic. Here, referred children were first seen and evaluated by a licensed clinical social worker or psychologist who had been trained in child and family therapy. Thorough assessments were conducted that included interviews with parents and teachers, and, most importantly, the evaluation included individual sessions with the child to determine their understanding of the reported difficulties. Staff psychiatrists provided consultation regarding a trial of medication only after a comprehensive assessment was completed and, except in rare circumstances, other interventions had been tried.

We can continue to study children's brains, and we can continue to medicate them so that they will conform, but there are significant potential costs to the child, particularly if the treatment is masking a different or more serious struggle. As well, children who learn to rely on medication may also learn that they can abdicate responsibility for their own behavior since they have been led to believe that it can only be controlled by medication. Brain studies are important, but the idea that they can explain all of what we see in our children is shortsighted, and potentially harmful.

Sally Satel, who is a psychiatrist and resident scholar at the American Enterprise Institute, and who specializes in the field of addictions, proposes that the increasing trend to reference brain studies to explain behavior is misleading. She notes that the changes in brain structure and function caused by repeated use of drugs and alcohol do not explain how addicts get sober because the mind and the brain are two different frameworks; while the neurobiological framework emphasizes the physical aspects that employ the mechanisms that drive thoughts and emotions, the mind emphasizes the sociological domain, which is about people's desires, intentions, ideals, and anxieties.

Therefore, it is the minds of addicts that best explain how addiction happens, why they continue to use and, if they decide to stop, how they manage *(Distinguishing Brain from Mind. The Atlantic*, 2013).

Studies of the brain should not be relied upon as the sole etiology for understanding behavior or to the exclusion of a broader analysis that includes psychosocial considerations. In our son's case, his indomitable determination and strong intellect supported his success in an environment that offered him increased flexibility and independence. A different child, who may also meet the diagnostic criteria for attention deficit hyperactivity disorder or oppositional defiant disorder, is likely to possess other attributes that may present as problematic in one setting but can find positive expression in another.

Recently, among the files that had accumulated relative to our son's journey, I discovered an application for a CHINS (Child in Need of Service Petition) to the state of Massachusetts which can, and often does, result in a youngster's transition into the Department of Youth Services, (mass.gov). Although the application had never been completed, it does reflect the mounting concern we felt about our son's increasingly serious transgressions with the law and our uncertainty regarding the best way to help him.

Hindsight provides clarity that is often inaccessible when life is happening. Today, it appears very clear that much of what our son, and we, experienced would not have happened at all had he been in a more flexible environment, but since we could not foresee that at the time, we had to rely on competent professional consultation and our own intuition And in the end, it was our intuition that allowed us to maintain our faith in the power of our son's positive qualities rather than to endorse a theory that focused primarily on those behaviors or attributes that were deemed to be inconvenient or problematic for others.

Sadly, we lost our oldest son to the ravages of his multiple handicaps in 2008. His disabilities were obvious, undeniable, and demanded specialized environmental support; yet, even with this level of disability, he was able to benefit from targeting the very few and subtle abilities he did possess. The lives of our two surviving children serve as a meaningful tribute to their brother's life, lending compelling credibility to the idea that we may get the best results with our children when we focus on their strengths and find ways to ensure that those strengths can find expression in their school environments.

IN HIS OWN WORDS

Excerpts from an interview, conducted by Brianne Carter, LICSW

How would you describe early years, your times with your brother and sister?

I used to get in trouble a lot with my little sister; we would argue, and things would escalate. She was the smarter one because she was able to quickly process a way to frame the argument so it was my fault, and they bought into it every time. Playing with my brother was always different. He lived with us for a period of time when we were all very young. I remember going to visit him when he began living in a pediatric nursing facility. That was always difficult for me, hospitals in general. It was difficult to see him and the other people he was with. They (the nursing facility) transported him to my middle school for a period of time. That was difficult too. Looking back, I'm sure kids that would make fun of him didn't mean anything by it. He would come once or twice a week and sit in with his aides in classes. I think that my mom knew it would be hard, but she knew that it was important for him, and I think it brought us closer together too.

Your mom talks about having a child with disabilities and how that puts everything else into perspective, (ear infections, not doing your homework). What did it mean for your perspective?

As a kid, I'm not really sure, but I think it planted the seed for my perspective now. You see people with

cerebral palsy that have a job and are pushing carts inside a grocery store, and it really bothers me when people who can walk and have full use of their arms and legs and their brain, especially in a country like this (with opportunity), and they don't use it. Having a brother like mine led to that perspective. I have little patience for people that don't have limitations like his; I'm probably a little more sensitive to people complaining who don't have a right to complain.

Do you think that contributed to the part of you that has strong self-determination, or to things that just don't matter, perhaps even things that you could recognize as arbitrary in the school system?

I don't think I was mature enough to have that vision at that age. I just knew it wasn't the right thing to force me, or any other kid, into a school that they didn't want to be in, one they hated and didn't get anything out of; so, at that point, anything else that went wrong, my attitude was, 'well that's not my problem because I never said that I wanted to be here anyway'. That's not an adult thing, right? That's kind of a kid thing, like, if I don't want to be here, and I get caught drinking in school, that's on you! One of the reasons that SVS worked for me is because, at some point, I realized that they weren't really asking me to do that much: show up, stay, and try to do something….When I started to get in trouble again at SVS, I think that's when I finally realized it's not everybody else's fault. Public school wasn't the right thing for me; it clearly works for a lot of *people. But once you took that (public school) out of the equation, then I started to realize where reality was. Maybe it's me.*

I'm fascinated by what might have been radically different for me should I have been put in a school where I had to decide for myself what I was interested in, how I was going to go about it. I'm very fascinated how that was just innate in you. I think your mom wants your voice in the mix. How did you experience SVS? Your mom said that, at SVS, you reconciled the issue of personal freedom with responsibility to the community.

There was an issue when I was almost expelled, and I was suspended for a period of time (within two months of being there). Some students and I went and smoked pot. I did the same thing at CCHS because I hated being there. But at SVS, they weren't really asking that much of me; it wasn't right for me to be doing that. I started to think longer term. I'm sure it says somewhere in psychology that when someone is faced with a limiting challenge (for me, public school) it becomes more difficult to think about the future; I began to think, what am I going to do with my life, and what is it going to take to get there? I wasn't as rebellious.

So that, if for the first 16 years of life you've been told what you should do and what you should want to do, and all of a sudden you have an opportunity to think about what you want to do, that's the pivotal moment when you decide that you don't want to smoke pot. It was never even something you necessarily wanted to do; it was just better than being beaten down and told what you wanted to do.

That's right.

Your mom's description didn't include that element, that once you remove all of the external factors you have to look at yourself, and, all of a sudden that affords you this sense of future. If the future that they painted for you is something that you don't want, then it may be difficult to feel that you do have a future.

That's exactly it. Somehow that helped me calibrate on reality. Taking away what CCHS thought my future should be, it kind of helped me calibrate on reality. I realized that I, partially, was the problem. Do I really want to be butting heads with people my entire life?

What was your level of awareness of the school system wanting to give you a diagnosis?

I remember it angering me; it's almost like blaming the victim. 'so (CCHS), you're going to force me into this program, and if I'm not complying, you're going to drug me so I will.

She talks about the smiley and frowny faces you came home with when you were little, and that most other kids didn't come home with, wondering if it felt like a label. Just before fourth grade, they wanted to look into ADHD. But your 4th grade teacher was a seminal change for you; do you remember him?

I do! Mr. Greene. He was jovial he made learning fun; his whole thing was about learning math through baseball, which I played at the time.

What appears to be a benefit for you is real life context rather than learning for learning sake. You liked baseball and it was relevant to life.

Even now, I work for a large corporation and, every year or two, we have to go through compliance training, things like 'what is harassment?' I have to sit there for a day and a half, and that feeling that I have sitting there is almost physically painful; it's the same way I used to feel in school. It had the same effect as learning the Spanish language or history. Now, I have an interest in those things, but I did not at that time.

Even at home, there was often conflict when you needed to do something you didn't want to do. Your mom describes having tried using a different approach at home after having consulted with a child psychologist. Do you remember that shift in your parent's approach? Was life easier at home?

I do remember the psychologist, but I don't remember the shift at home.

Did home feel distinct from school, as to how you were seen and allowed to be, even when there were moments of confrontation?

I'm sure I felt that I was more understood, but in school you can't expect a teacher to have the same understanding when they have 200 kids coming through every year. You can't compensate (at home) for what kids experience at school.

How would you describe yourself? How did you hold onto that sense of yourself?

I've completed that, 'What's Your Work Style?' and I'm firmly a 'Driver'. I like to go and get things done; it almost doesn't matter what it is; I like to own what's going on. I like my career in sales because it's up to you to go close the deal no matter what challenges you face; I thrive on that. The difference now, from when I was I kid, is that I realize that I'm not always right. I still have that same 'I'm going to figure out how to get it done' mentality, but I realize that someone else may know more than I do.

Somehow, you protected your sense of self by your thought process at the time ('It's your problem, not mine'). They tried to diagnose you with ODD, but you held onto your sense of self by saying that it's their fault.

The calibration in my thinking took place at SVS rather than when I was 24 yrs. old and out in the real world. An intervention creates a false rock bottom for an addict; that's what SVS was for me, a false rock bottom.

Had you not had that change in your thought process, I'm even wondering if you would have gotten to that age of 24?

I was getting worse and worse by the week. I didn't respect teacher's authority. There was a time that I got brought home by the police, and I didn't particularly respect his authority either.

Do you equate your anger with the quote "Many boys become more and more angry about all of the things they're expected to do – things that make no sense to them and seem like a waste of time?" Many adolescents feel that way, but I feel like it was within your ethics.

That is the way it was and I don't know why. When I was 18, I got a draft card (you have to register for the draft), and I was furious about that. I just didn't like being told what to do. It was like a philosophical belief for me. It was more than (that) I just wanted to screw around and have fun. It's a problem that gets worse as you get older; as an adolescent, you want to make your own way in the world, and school started to feel more and more like a prison.

Your mother equates the loss of other high school students with the loss of your brother, not necessarily in terms of suicide, but the possibility of losing you, who you are. She could have lost you both, and how needless that would have been, losing your brother to natural circumstances and the possibility of losing you to an environment you were in. Do you ever credit SVS with saving your life? Did it ever get that dire?

It's tough to really know what would have happened had I not gone to SVS. It was like a false rock bottom (here's reality; you got what you wanted; now what). It's highly possible that, had I not had that as a teenager and figured it out then, it would have happened at a later point in life when it was too late; maybe I wouldn't have been able to respond, react, and change my thinking if it had happened in my twenties or later. I have used the phrase 'it saved my life' a lot of times. People don't get it. I remember telling a coworker (she was in her 30's or 40's); that I was going to a different school now with no formal classes. There are teachers, but they're not really teaching you, and she laughed in my face. To people like that, I would say, 'you laugh, but it saved my life'.

If you hadn't had the opportunity to dissipate that anger, I'm wondering about what kind of relationships you would have missed out on, maybe with your parents or even your sister? I think you are saying that SVS not only allowed you to find and preserve your own career path, but you got to channel all of your constitutional qualities in the right way, and you got to have relationships, both with authority and your peers. Clearly, there's something about emotional health and feeling connected to other people, including authority, which you never felt at CCHS.

*That's absolutely true. At SVS, you can't do whatever you want. It's interpreted that way, but you can't as I found out by walking off campus to smoke pot. But there's a whole judicial system that is set up the same way our judicial system is in real life, which is that there are laws and if you become aware of someone breaking a rule, you can 'bring them up', and people took it seriously. You can accuse someone by pressing charges, and there's a hearing. There was a counsel; students would make a decision, and staff was involved as well. It was modeled after our own judicial system, which is clearly better, involving the students in the whole process. It's '101' for how **not** to make someone feel alienated. There was a school meeting, including judicial committee every Thursday, and the room was always packed. The kids would show up and plead their case; it got into what is right, and what should be right. You'd probably be surprised at how seriously the students were about it.*

Is this how you resolve arguments in your house now?

No, I just do what I'm told. My wife accuses me of trying to "sell" her. My idea of selling is to try to logically lead someone to what, I think, is the right answer.

You're authentically stating your perspective. It speaks to the success of how you've preserved who you are, not only channeled in your work; but it's so authentic to you that it's also within your personal relationships. There's not really a difference between the two; there's no false presentation.

I sell enterprise software to CIO/CEO types with a lot more experience than I have. Many co-workers are intimidated by those that are more experienced than they are, but I've never had a problem with that; I always treat them as my equal. It's funny; it never backfires. They never take exception to my treating them like a peer.

Given your experience in the educational system, as it still stands, what would you do with your own kid; how would you approach his or her education?

I don't know at this point. Is SVS right for everyone or was it just right for me? If I had a child that was like me, then I think sending them to SVS at some point is something I would definitely consider. Some kids go there for their entire education, starting when they're five or six, until they graduate. I don't know that I would necessarily jump to that. Do you think it's something that is maybe right for everyone? Do you think my mom is saying that it is? It's tough because, obviously, each parent has his or her own child's best interest in mind. I would think that there are more options today; in-between options. There are many people who did just fine after graduation from SVS; I'm not the only one. I think it was the right answer for many students.

REFERENCE LIST

Ackoff, R. L., & Greenberg, D. A. (2008). *Turning learning right side up: putting education back on track.* Upper Saddle River, NJ: Prentice Hall.

Acosta, R. M. & Hutchinson, M. (2017, January 7). They raise the world's happiest children – so is it time you went Dutch? *The Telegraph, 1-11.*

American Psychiatric Association. (2013). *Diagnostic and statistical manual of mental disorders* (5th ed.). Washington, DC.

Brown, T. E. (2013, April). The truth about ADHD. *Psychology Today.* https://www.psychologytoday.com/blog/the-mysteries-add/201304/

Arnett, J. J. (2010). *Adolescence and emerging adulthood: a cultural approach (4th ed.).* Boston, MA: Prentice Hall.

Centers for Disease Control and Prevention [CDC], 2017). ADHD Homepage Data and Statistics.

Cha, A. E. (2016, May 3). CDC warns that Americans may be overmedicating youngest children with ADHD. *The Washington Post.*

Chess, S. & Thomas, A. (1987). *Know your child: An authoritative guide for today's parents.* New York, NY: Basic Books.

Clikeman, M. (2005, November/December). Neuropsychological aspects for evaluating learning disabilities. *Journal of Learning Disabilities* 38, 563-568.

Dobson, J. (2004). *The new strong-willed child.* Wheaton, IL: Tyndale House.
Faber, A., Coe, K. A., & Mazlish, E. (2012). *Siblings without rivalry: how to help your children live together so you can live too.* New York, NY: W.W. Norton.

Featherstone, H. (1981). *A difference in the family: living with a disabled child.* Middlesex, England: Penguin Books.

Gopnik, A. (2009). *The philosophical baby: what children's minds tell us about truth, love, and the meaning of life.* New York, NY: Farrar, Straus and Giroux.

Gray, P. (2013). *Free to learn: why unleashing the instinct to play will make our children happier, more self-reliant, and better students for life.* New York, NY: Basic Books.

Gray, P. and Feldman, J. (2004). Playing in the zone of proximal development: qualities of self-directed age mixing between adolescents and young children at a democratic school. *The University of Chicago Press Journals University of Chicago Press Books.* Volume 110, Number 21.

Gray, P., and Chernoff, D. (1986). Democratic schooling: What happens to young people who have charge of their own education? *American Journal of Education*, 94, pp.182-213. doi:10-1086/443842.

Greene, R. W. (2014). *Lost at school: why our kids with behavioral challenges are falling through the cracks and how we can help them*. New York, NY: Scribner.

Greene, R. W. (2010). *The explosive child: a new approach for understanding and parenting easily frustrated, chronically inflexible children*. New York, NY: Harper Paperbacks.

Greenberg, D. (2001). An op ed piece. *Metrowest Daily News*. Framingham, MA.

Greenberg, D. (2016). *A place to grow: the culture of Sudbury Valley School*. Framingham, MA: Sudbury Valley School Press.

Greenberg, D., Sadofsky, M., and Lempka, J. (2005). *The pursuit of happiness: the lives of Sudbury valley alumni*. Framingham, MA: Sudbury Valley School Press.

Halverson C., Kohnstamm, G.A. & Martin, R.P. (1994). *The developing structure of temperament and personality from infancy to adulthood*. Mahwah, NJ: Lawrence Erlbaum Associates.

Hinshaw, S. P. & Scheffler, R. M. (2014). *The ADHD explosion: myths, medication, money and today's push for performance*. New York, NY: Oxford University Press.

Hoogman, et al. (2017). Subcortical brain volume differences of participants with ADHD across the across

the lifespan: an ENIGMA collaboration.
http://www.thelancet.com/journals/lanpsy/article/PIIS221
5-0366(17)300494/

Hughes, S. (2017, March/April). Pressure & Proof. *The Pennsylvania Gazette*, 38-45.

Jenco, M. (2017/February) Study: Brain difference found in children with ADHD *AAP News*, 1-3.

Kendall, P.C., & Braswell, L. (1982). Cognitive-behavioral self-control therapy for children: A components analysis. *Journal of Consulting and Clinical Psychology*, 50(5), 672-689.

Linkletter, A. (1957). *Kids say the darndest things*. Upper Saddle River, NJ: Prentice Hall.

Matthys,W. & Lochman, J. E. (2010). *Oppositional Defiant Disorder and conduct disorder in childhood.* Chichester, West Sussex, UK.

McClowry, S., & Collins, A. (2012). Temperament-based intervention: reconceptualized from a response to intervention framework. In R. Shiner, & M. Zentner (Eds.*), Handbook of childhood temperament* (pp. 607-626). New York, NY: Guilford Press.

McClowry, S.G et al. (2009). Testing the efficacy of INSIGHTS on student disruptive behavior, classroom management, and student competence in inner city primary grades. *School Mental Health.* Https://www.ncbinim.nih.gov/pmc/articles/PMC2830583/

Miller, P. (2003, September 6). Think Your Dog Has ADHD? *Whole Dog Journal.* https://www.whole-dog-journal.com/behavior/think-your-dog-has-adhd/

Nutt, A. E. (2017). Attention Deficit/Hyperactivity Disorder is linked to delayed brain development. *The Washington Post.*

Rothbart, M. K. (2011). *Becoming who we are: temperament and personality in development.* New York, NY: Guilford Press.

Ruf, D.L. (2005). *Losing our minds: gifted children left behind.* Tucson, AZ: Great Potential Press.

Sasse, B. (2017, May6). Perpetual adolescence and what to do about it. *Wall Street Journal.*

Satel, S. (2013, May). Distinguishing brain from mind. *The Atlantic, 3-7.*

Schrank, F.A., Mather, N., & McGrew, K.S. (2014). Woodcock –Johnson Achievement Test

Schwartz, A. (2016). *ADHD nation: children, doctors, big pharma, and the making of an American epidemic.* New York, NY: Scribner.

Semrud-Clikeman, M. (2005, November/December). Neuropsychological aspects for evaluating learning disabilities. *Journal of Learning Disabilities Volume 38, Number 6. pp.563-568.*

Shiner, et al. (2012). What is Temperament Now? Assessing Progress in Temperament Research on the Twenty-Fifth Anniversary of Goldsmith et al. (1987). *Child Development Perspectives: Volume 0, Number 0, pp 1-9.*

Smith, M. (2017, January 17). Hyperactive around the world? The history of ADHD in global perspective. *Social History of Medicine.*

Spencer, K. (2017, April 5). It takes a suburb: a town struggles to ease student stress. *New York Times.*

United Health Foundation (2020) *Health of Women and Children, americashealthrankings.org (2019).*

Vgotsky, L. (2003*). Educational Theory in Cultural Context.* New York, NY: Cambridge University Press.

Webb, et al. (2004). *Misdiagnosis and dual diagnosis of gifted children and adults: ADHD, Bipolar, OCD, Asperger's, Depression, and other disorders. Tucson, AZ.:* Great Potential Press.

Wedge, M. (2015). *A disease called childhood: why ADHD became an American epidemic.* New York, NY: Avery.

Wedge, M. (2011). *Suffer the children: the case against labeling and medicating and an effective alternative.* New York, NY: W.W. Norton & Company.

Wedge, M. (2012). Why French Kids Don't Have ADHD. https:///www.psychologytoday.com/blog/suffer-the-children/201203/.

ABOUT THE AUTHOR

Claire T. Russell is a Licensed Clinical Social Worker and former school teacher. She was the Director of Children's Services at Community Healthlink, a regional mental health agency in Central Massachusetts and the former Director of Developmental Disabilities at Cambridge Children and Family Services, also in Massachusetts. During her career, she developed a school-based services program that provided on-site clinical services for children, adolescents and teachers in more than a dozen area school districts. She wrote this book in order to promote further understanding about the inseparable connection between conventional educational practices and current trends in children's mental health.